C000170908

BLOCKCHAIN, BITCOIN AND YOU

by Temple Melville

BLOCKCHAIN, BITCOIN
AND YOU

TEMPLE MELVILLE
WITH DANETTE WALLACE

BLOCKCHAIN, BITCOIN AND YOU.
Written by Temple Melville
Contributions by Danette Wallace, Sudhir Khatwani and
Brian Mackay
Published by The Magic Road
Edinburgh

First published in 2021

The moral rights of the author have been asserted.

Production Manager: Peter Burnett
Contributing Editor: Joshua Andrew

The Magic Road. is an imprint of
Leamington Books
32 Leamington Terrace
Edinburgh

Typeset in Garamond and Bebas Neue Bold

Cover design by Cavan Convery
ISBN 9781914090141

Picture a spreadsheet that is duplicated thousands of times across a network of computers. Then imagine that this network is designed to regularly update this spreadsheet and you have a basic understanding of the blockchain.

CONTENTS

APPENDICES

INTRODUCTION

When Satoshi Nakamoto produced his white paper *Bitcoin: A Peer-to-Peer Electronic Cash System* in 2009, he can have had no idea what he was unleashing on an unsuspecting world. I would have to say not only was the world unsuspecting, it was also largely uncaring!

With everything else moving at the speed of light in the world of technology, some may feel that the whole Bitcoin and Blockchain thing just suddenly arrived on the scene out of nowhere, but, as ever, the truth is somewhat different.

What we now think of as the blockchain in fact emerged from work that Linux programmers carried out in the late 1990's and early 2000's. What they were doing was producing robust and quickly developing coding by using thousands of programmers and coders all over the world. It's true that English is the language of the internet, but some of these people didn't speak English. What they did speak was code.

One problem that these coders solved concerned both the duplication of work and what we call 'version control'. How did Mr.A in Norway know that Mr. B in South

America hadn't already done that bit of work? The answer is that all the code had to be ranked by time. So if Mr. A did some work at 9:05:45 that fact was broadcast to everyone who was working on the problem. As a result they were able to tell what the very very latest version was, and so there was no duplication and work progressed in a linear fashion rather than disjointedly.

This was the basis of Satoshi's thinking. If everyone had the information at the instant it was available, that meant that 'cheating' or changing any of that information, was almost impossible. If fifty people were told a thing, then to change that thing meant you had to get fifty people to change their minds, and you then had to change the information that was in the fifty people's inbox.

This of course is an oversimplification, but I think you can see the point.

Satoshi's next brilliant insight was to say: maybe you don't need all fifty people to agree, maybe you only need twenty-six out of the fifty. As a result, the system Satoshi proposed showed that as long as more than 50% agreed a solution, that solution could be taken as true. In reality, if the solution goes to all fifty users at once it is extremely unlikely anyone is going to be a naysayer.

The next aspect which Satoshi Nakamoto's paper addressed related to was what was happening in the world of traditional finance at that time. Trust in banks, their ability to be the guardians of the ledgers, and trust in other financial institutions was at an all-time low. If — Satohsi's paper suggested — there could be an alternative payment mechanism that didn't have any interference from traditional bankers, then the world might be a better place. What was needed, the paper suggested, was a system of decentralised confirmation, not one-point confirmation. But there was a problem — and this problem which is called the Double Spend problem, is only related to money.

The thing is, we can re-create anything digitally. It's why e-Books and downloads for music exist. You want them identical – that's why we are buying them. You don't want a different ending of the song you download to the one you just heard on the radio, and the quality must be, and is with digital, the same evey time. Being the same is no use for money though. The £1 in your pocket or bank account is inherently different from the one in mine. There's a wonderful skit that Tony Hancock did when he deposited a £5 note into his bank then decided to take it out again. Of course, he got back a note that didn't have his signature on it. So it wasn't 'his'. And he was absolutely right – it wasn't his. It had a different number on it.

And that, Ladies and Gentlemen, is the problem. Digitally they would be identical — although for a system of money to work, we need them to be different.

Satoshi's brilliance was to create conditions whereby each string of code WAS different. This meant that, having been created, the code was broadcast to all the computers that were on the system instantly. This meant that anyone looking at the current state of the code could be sure it was correct. At the same time, the bit of code that had been allocated to each individual was unique to them, and locked into place.

And this book will explain how that all happens.

A BRIEF HISTORY OF DIGITAL CURRENCY

Twenty years ago, the internet gave us the means to freely exchange information. Today blockchain technology allows us to freely exchange value. Society is about to be utterly transformed again.

A bold statement, you may say. What we will see over the course of this book, however, is that if anything, this is an understatement. The truth is that the impact that this new technology will have and the actual outcomes may be even more radical than we or anyone can predict. This is truly disruptive technology.

Why do alternative currencies exist?

To a large extent, Altcoins are an expression of the times that spawned them. An Altcoin is an alternative digital currency to Bitcoin, and in practice, the term ultimately refers to all the cryptocurrencies other than Bitcoin.

At a time when trust in banks, regulatory authorities and capitalism was at an all-time low, the lure of being able to trade without using any of the foregoing as intermediaries was instantly attractive. Lehman Bros collapse precipitated a rash of mergers and rescues, not least of which in the UK was Royal Bank of Scotland. To this day (and perhaps forever) the money put into the bank by the British Government remains awaiting repayment.

So a system where neither banks nor governments could interfere with transfers, a system where the value of that transfer was entirely independent and could not be interfered with — had people clamouring to know more. Remember that, in the previous financial crash, in some cases deposits were wiped out. In Ireland whole sectors of the economy disappeared. In Cyprus, the government simply wrote off deposits and debentures to make the banks whole again. People did not want to lose what they had.

In a sense, Satoshi Nakamoto was pushing at an open door when he published his white paper. Even although it took time to become widely considered as a realistic possibility, upon the release of Bitcoin: A Peer-to-Peer Electronic Cash System in 2009, people immediately realised they could make money out of their own coins. And so, because of this, the ICO (Initial Coin Offering) was born. The ICO offered entrepreneurs the chance to retain 100% of the upside while still funding their dream. What this meant in practice was that funds could be raised for any purpose, by the creation of cryptocurrencies.

The history of alternative currencies

The WIR Franc is an electronic currency issued by the WIR Bank, which is reflected in the bank's clients' trade accounts. Crucially, with this currency, there is no paper money. When the WIR Franc was first issued, it was intended that the currency would increase sales and reduce the costs of cash flow, and so result in increased profits for the qualified participants. At first, the WIR Bank created a credit system which issued credit, in WIR Francs, to its members. Then the credit lines were secured by members pledging assets which ensured that the currency was asset-backed. The result is that when two members enter into a transaction with both Swiss Francs and WIR Francs, this reduces the amount of cash needed by the buyer, and the seller does not discount its product or service.

WIR was founded in 1934 by businessmen Werner Zimmermann and Paul Enz and it was created as a result of currency shortages and global financial instability. A banking license was granted in 1936. Both Zimmermann and Enz had been influenced by German libertarian socialist economist Silvio Gesell; however, the WIR Bank renounced Gesell's 'free money' theory in 1952, opening the door to monetary interest.

'WIR' is both an abbreviation of *Wirtschaftsring* and the word for 'we' in German, reminding participants that the economic circle is also a community. According to the cooperative's statutes, "Its purpose is to encourage participating members to put their buying power at each other's disposal and keep it circulating within their ranks, thereby providing members with additional sales volume."

Although WIR started with only sixteen members, today it has grown to include 70,000. The total assets of the bank are approximately CHF 3.0 billion , and annual sales were in the range of CHF 6.5 billion, as long ago as 2005. As of 1998, assets held by the credit system were 885 million with at the same time, liabilities amounting to 844 million — that means that the circulating WIR money, with equity in the system, was in the region of 44 million. These WIR Bank obligations, being interest free, have a cost of zero. Income from interest and credit clearing activities were 38 million francs.

The WIR Bank was a not-for-profit entity, although that status changed during the bank's expansion. The bank considers themselves as stable, and claim that they are fully operational during times of general economic crisis and that their activity may also dampen downturns in the business cycle, helping to stabilise the Swiss economy during difficult times.

Bitcoin history

In January 2009 a person or persons using the pseudonym Satoshi Nakamoto published a ground-breaking paper *Bitcoin – A Peer-to-Peer Electronic Cash System* — and very few people noticed. The proposed project utilised a technology that has come to be known as blockchain, combining strong cryptography and linked lists. It drew on work by the Linux development team which had previously managed to develop a system which allowed people from all over the world to combine on the marvellous code that we know as Linux.

A few months after the Satoshi Nakamoto white paper the first release of the Bitcoin code took place — but again very few people outside the tech world and early adopters took notice. Bitcoin was nothing more than a hobby at this stage, an experiment in new ways to transfer value.

Over the course of the next few years Bitcoin would slowly gain more attention from the general public. Shrouded in mystery, Bitcoin would often be referenced in hacking and cybercrime articles in the media. This perhaps undeserved infamy helped to draw more attention to Bitcoin and lead others to examine the source code.

One of the more interesting moments in Bitcoin's early history took place on 22nd May, 2010. This was when the first known commercial transaction involving Bitcoin took place, in which a Florida man paid for two pizzas with the cryptocurrency. The day has become part of digital folklore, not just because of the transaction, but because the price: the man in question paid 10,000 Bitcoins for the two pizzas which today is worth over four million dollars. This is now known as Bitcoin Pizza Day — and on that day Laszlo Hanyecz agreed to pay 10,000 Bitcoins for two delivered Papa John's pizzas. Organised on a bitcoin forum, the Florida man reached out for help. "I'll pay 10,000 bitcoins for a couple of pizzas so I have some left over for the next day," Hanyecz wrote.

A British man took up Hanyecz's offer and bought the two pizzas for him in exchange for the 10,000 Bitcoins. Since the inception of Bitcoin, Hanyeczs' pizzas have become more and more expensive. Nine months after the purchase Bitcoin reached parity with the US dollar making the two pizzas worth $10,000 and in 2015, the fifth anniversary of Bitcoin Pizza Day, the two pizzas were valued at $2.4 million.

Thanks to the open source ethos, which makes significant amounts of code publically available, thousands across the globe came to realise the potential this technology had and quickly began to create their own versions of Bitcoin. These were called *altcoins*.

Many of these altcoins rose to prominence, with some created just for fun like Dogecoin, or others such as Litecoin which aimed for faster block times using a different cryptographic algorithms.

In Scotland, Scotcoin was launched at the tail end of 2013 and distributed in early 2014 by Derek Nisbet, an IT specialist operating in the financial sector. Many hard lessons were learnt regarding security and the need for a team approach. Scotcoin transferred to the CounterParty protocol (of which more later) in late 2014 and in 2015 control and ownership of the project passed to the present team. Scotcoin has flourished and looks forward to a bright future indeed.

Also in Scotland, during 2017, the first real estate sale conducted in cryptocurrency took place in Glasgow.

Some of the global enterprises that now accept Bitcoin as payment include Paypal, Microsoft, Mozilla the developers of the Firefox browser, Expedia, Greenpeace, and Dell.

Banks and financial institutions are now working hard to embrace and extend cryptocurrencies and blockchain technology in general. Again — more of this later.

There is however in the meantime a certain lack of understanding and knowledge of this nascent technology with only a few thousand people estimated, able to truly comprehend it.

OVERVIEW OF TRADITIONAL BANKING

Traditional banking has served us well for centuries but is far from perfect. Transactions between banks can take days to clear and human eyes are needed on every transaction.

Costs are naturally high.

Cryptocurrencies on the other hand offer significantly faster transactions at a tiny fraction of the costs and opportunities for fraud are vastly reduced. Crypto-currencies have no concept of borders and costs are the same whether sending currency to Stirling or Shenyang, Newton Mearns or New York

However, the Bitcoin blockchain is able to verify less than a dozen transactions per second, whereas credit card processors can verify up to 70,000 per second.

Obviously, the current implementation of the blockchain requires further work before it can challenge traditional methods. A fierce debate is taking place within the community of developers as to the best way forward — and some innovative and promising proposals are being tested right now.

To understand why the Blockchain is different to traditional banking it's important to understand how traditional fractional-reserve banking works. The system of fractional-reserve banking is the most common practised by commercial banks worldwide and originated many centuries ago, when bankers realised that not all their despositers would require their money at the same time. This means that when £100 invested by you or me into Bank 1 – they keep 10% and loan out 90% to Bank 2 to lend to its customers. Bank 2 then loans 90% to Bank 3, keeping back the 10% reserve they have to keep as collateral —and so on down the chain.

This is all recorded manually, on different databases and each Bank has its own system. Notwithstanding faster payments, it can take up to three days of checking to clear the funds from one ledger to another — and that delay increases the chances of fraud creeping in.

What, for example happens if the £100 initially put in to Bank 1 is made up fake £20 notes? Or what happens if Bank 2 lends to someone who can't pay their loan back, and Bank 3 has already lent the cash out? What if one of the Banks collapses? This happened in 2008 and there is a continued likelihood of similar events in the future, despite the additional capital requirements and additional oversights that have been put in place since then.

The technology of the blockchain allows digital information to be distributed, but not copied. That means each individual piece of data can only have one owner.

One of the strongest points in favour of cryptocurrencies is that they are decentralised. Our present fiat system (banks, credit cards etc.) relies on a middleman. When you buy something in a shop the seller relies on the fact that when your card is cleared, they will get paid by a trusted third party — the bank.

From the bank's point of view, they have to do a massive amount of work to make sure that firstly, you are who you say you are and that secondly the money you want to pay with has not been fraudulently obtained. Further, this trusted third party, the bank, has to make sure that either you have the money in your account or at least the ability to repay the bank if necessary. All this costs billions, and is a single point of attack. It's also why bank charges are so high. The banks have to cover the billions and billions that are stolen every year. If they didn't, they would no longer be trusted third parties. Banks are entirely involved in every aspect of everyone's finance and also their identity, and they have to know everything about you to be able to track fraudulent borrowers or lenders. This is especially true because physical money (and banking protocols) can be counterfeited, credit cards can be cloned or stolen and wrongfully charged or reversed.

Imagine two entities, such as banks, that need to update their own user account balances when there is a request to transfer money from one customer to another. These entities need to spend a tremendous amount of time and effort coordinating, synchronising, messaging and checking to ensure that each transaction happens exactly as it should. Typically, to ensure the most amount of safety for all, the money being transferred is held by the originator until it can be confirmed that it was received by the recipient. With the blockchain, a single ledger of transaction entries that both parties have access to can simplify the coordination and validation efforts because there is always a single version of records, not two disparate databases.

On the blockchain, there is no central authority holding all that information. There doesn't need to be. There doesn't need to be a third party standing in the middle tearing their hair out as they try to make sure it's all legitimate. Peer to peer means just that. Person A provides a service to Person B who pays PersonA directly. It means there is no security problem with the data being held in a single point of contact, because it's spread throughout the system over thousands of nodes — which just means computers, really. Once the transaction has been confirmed, that's it. One of the really good things about the blockchain is the transaction cannot be reversed. That means that the old excuse "The cheque is in the post" is actually true.

BITCOIN AND BLOCKCHAIN RELATIONSHIP

We have looked at central banking, let's now turn to an overview of the Blockchain and its relationship to Bitcoin. We'll try not to go into too many of the technical aspects, but some learning is necessary.

And first we should start by saying that Bitcoin and the Blockchain are two distinct things.

A blockchain can exist without Bitcoin, but Bitcoin could not exist without its blockchain. The Blockchain is an enabling technology, and Bitcoin is only one application of it. There can be an unlimited number of blockchains, but in general usage, when people speak of 'The Blockchain' they are referring to the blockchain used by Bitcoin.

So, what is the Blockchain?

A blockchain is a method of recording data —-a distributed digital ledger or database of transactions, agreements, contracts — any kind of data that needs to be independently recorded and verified as having happened.

The big difference between this ledger and a traditonal

ledger is that this ledger isn't stored in one place — it's distributed across several thousands of nodes around the world. But in essence it performs in exactly the same way as the big paper bank ledgers of old did. When Person A transfers £10 to Person B, the ledger moves £10 from Person A's account and adds it to Person B's. Very straightforward — and as I say, in function the same as it's always been.

The clever bit is that once that has been recorded, it can't be erased, altered or changed in any way. The reason for this is because the transaction is not held in one place like on the old ledger. Instead, the information is sent instantly to all the computers on the system, so that everyone everywhere can see it has happened.

It's like an enormous number of notaries being present at every transaction, and every one of them accessible from anywhere on the Internet.

Think about that — a notary present at every transaction with their affidavit being instantly available to everyone, and incontestable.

Why Blockchain is so useful

What follows is an oversimplification — but for the purposes of explanation it will still be useful.

A blockchain implementation consists of two parts — and these are two separate but linked sets of data. The transaction — for example some Bitcoin transferring from A to B — is the first part. The second part is what I would describe as 'comments' or 'notes.' Transactions are the actual data stored on the blockchain. In the notes will be stored other information. Blocks in the chain record and confirm when and in what sequence transactions became written into the chain — and they exist as part of the blockchain.

The central point here is the two-step nature of what happens. It means you can effectively piggyback a huge amount of information and data onto a transaction of minimal proportions.

For example, take a £5 note. You can turn the note into a cheque or an IOU by simply writing "Pay Mr. Melville £10,000" on it. You then sign it and put your bank sort code and account number on it. You might have to wait while things were verified, but if there are funds, the bank will honour it. But think of this: You could simply spend the £5. Not the best commercial decision, but you could do it. On the blockchain, if you send the tiny bit of coin, you are effectively sending all the data attached to it as well — in this case the fact that £10,000 is available.

There are lots of uses for this unique characteristic. A company called Everledger has started tracking diamonds by uisng a blockchain. All the data about a particular diamond can be added to a transaction and it will be stored forever. If stolen, the rightful owner can show — absolutely and without any doubt — that they are the owner.

You can transfer and more importantly track any physical or digital itemising the unmodifiable recording properties of a blockchain. It can be done with patents, music copyright, writing a book, part ownership of artworks, cars, bottles of whisky — in fact just about anything you can think of. Provenance in art is everything. Here you have the entire provenance certified and immutably lodged for all time.

In fact, there is an unfortunate child somewhere out there who has had her birth and birth details forever made visible to everyone worldwide. This is because her father put her birth and everything to do with it onto a Bitcoin transaction a few years ago. That's just one way the Blockchain could be used to speed up and make sure the data is properly recorded and available to view.

Conditions for using blockchain in your business

The following checklist is sourced from the Forrester Research report. Forrester are the leading research and trusted authority for all IT and they specialise in blockchain matters:

* Do multiple parties need to access the same datat or write to the data source?

* Do all the parties need assurance that the data is valid and hasn't been tampered with?

* Do you rely on an intermediary that adds no value? Or do you rely on a complex unreliable process to reconcile the transactions of multiple parties — when all should have the same data? Or is there no system available today that does what you require?

* Are there good reasons not to have a centralised system?

If the answer to all of these questions is "yes" — then it is worth considering a blockchain solution, provided that the difficulty you've identified is shared by other ecosystem players, or you have identified partners that are interested in exploring a new opportunity with you.

If you can tick all these boxes then you can probably save some serious sums of money by implementing a blockchain solution

Security

One of the most common questions people ask is: "How safe is the blockchain?"

There are several layers to the response.

Firstly, in order for a transaction to be verified, the answer to an extremely complex mathematical equation has to be approved by all the nodes.

In other words, one node gets to the answer first — and that node wins a prize — but that node does not win until everyone else in the system agrees with it.

It's no use simply saying the answer is wrong, because, if it is manifestly correct, there is nothing to be gained by not agreeing. It is in the interests of all to get the equation correct first, and to get it right. Once it has been agreed, that solution is signed, sealed and delivered into a sealed block and can not — and for all practical purposes can never be changed.

That's layer one.

However, this block could in theory be changed, but only if every single block is changed right from the beginning, which in the case of the Bitcoin Blockchain is coming on for nearly 700,000 blocks. The problem is if you change something in block 699,999, that automatically means the summarised output — called the 'hash' — from block 699,998 has to be changed, because if it does not, then the 'sums' for 699,999 won't add up. And if you change that one, you have to change the hash that 'seeded' 699,997 — and so on right the way back to Block 1. Clearly, such a massive undertaking would be very difficult.

That's layer two.

The third layer is a conceptual one, and requires some mathematical thought.

How difficult is it to make those changes from layer two? People often say that it is something like trying to find a single identifiable, certain grain of sand in the desert — but it is in fact even more difficult than that. It is in fact even more diffciult than looking for that particular grain amongst *all* the grains of sand in the world. And just to add a bit of spice to it, let's say that grain has had all its characteristics registered on a certain block, so you would alos need to check each block at this level of complexity

Not secure enough? OK, let's say all the grains of sand or dust in the Solar System?

You want more?

Take it up another level — one grain of any matter you like, in the entire Solar System.

That might do it, but if you are really and truly worried about security, we should go up another level.

Let us say that the complexity of the problem we need to solve in order to change the block records is equivalent to finding one grain among ALL the grains of sand, all the dust, all the molecules, all the atoms, neutrons — and in fact, everything there is in the entire universe.

I think that might just be secure enough.

And in fact, the belief is that it's mathematically more difficult than even that.

Governments and digital currency

How do I account for my digital currencies in my tax return?

As ever with an asset class there are two ways you can make money. One is to buy and sell it on a regular basis, hopefully making a profit, which classifies you as a trader. Alternatively, as with any other asset, you can buy it and hold for a long period. If you sell what you bought for more than you paid for it, that means you have made a capital gain. These two different gains are taxed slightly differently, but no differently than if you were buying and selling paintings, or a property. It's a similar situation. You have to pay capital gains tax on the profit. On the trading side, you pay tax on the basis of the profit you earn in a given period.

As of now, the United States Internal Revenue Service has been busily reminding people that they need to pay tax on their earnings or gains. In 2016(?) only around 50 people in the States paid tax on crypto earnings. This year I have a feeling there will be lots more. People will begin to feel that the IRS are taking more notice of sums of money that have hitherto been ignored. In the UK, the HMRC has been entirely consistent. Cryptocurrency is treated in exactly the same way as foreign exchange. As of now the FCA (Financial Conduct Authority) is registering any company connected with crypto and digital currency — and a good thing too.

Government adoption — why are they interested?

Governments around the world are ambivalent about cryptocurrencies. They all think blockchain is wonderful, but are not so keen on digital currencies. Countries where people want to get cash out of the country are of course enitrely against them — India and China are good examples. Even so, the Chinese authorities are keen on Bitcoin mining. — or at least they were until they realised that their own digital Yuan needed space to grow in its own home market.

Meanwhile, the British authorities are doing their best to ignore the situation and the Americans — of course — are holding Congressional hearings. Longer term, however, blockchains are going to be able to assist governments with many things. One example might be the use of blockchain technology by the NHS (National Health Service) in the UK. The NHS has dozens of different IT systems that they have been trying to amalgamate at the cost of billions of pounds. If they had started by building a blockchain solution, and then transferring the data to that, this amalgamtion would have been finished by now and would have been very much cheaper.

BLOCKCHAIN BASICS

In this chapter, Bitcoin and blockchain technology will be explained. It's not as easy to do that as you might think, and there are several ways in, as well as many different analgies and examples that can be considered.

Here is a start, however: what if there's a technological advancement so powerful that it transforms the principal pillars of our society? A technology which fundamentally influences the way that our economy, governance systems and businesses function, and could change our conceptual understanding of trade, ownership and trust?

This technology already exists and it's called cryptocurrency.

People often think of Bitcoin as only virtual money or a transaction system, but if you look closer you'll see that the monetary aspect is just the tip of the iceberg. That's because Bitcoin is a ground-breaking internet technology for which money is merely one of the possible applications.

Money exists to facilitate trade — and through the centuries trade has become incredibly complex. Everyone trades with everyone worldwide; trade is recorded in book-keeping and this information is often isolated and closed to the public. For this reason we use third parties which we trust to facilitate and approve our transactions. Think of governments, banks, accountants, notaries and the paper money in your wallet. We call these 'Trusted Third Parties.'

This brings us to the essence of Bitcoin. Bitcoin software enables a network of computers to maintain a collective book-keeping ledger via the internet. This system of book-keeping is neither closed nor in control of one party. Rather, it is public and available in one digital ledger which is fully distributed across the network. We call this the 'Blockchain.'

In the Blockchain, all transactions are logged including information on the time, date, participants and amount of every single transaction. Each node in the network owns a full copy of the Blockchain, and for the Blockchain to be an accurate and valid record or ledger, all of these copies must match. On the basis of complicated state of the art mathematical principles the transactions are verified by the so called Bitcoin miners who maintain the ledger. The mathematical principles also ensure that these notes automatically and continuously agree about the current state of the ledger and every transaction in it. If anyone attempts to corrupt the transaction, the nodes will not arrive at a consensus and hence will refuse to incorporate the transaction into the Blockchain. This means that every transaction is public and that thousands of nodes unanimously agree that a transaction has occurred at date X at time Y. It's almost like there's a notary present at every transaction. This way, everyone has access to a shared single source of truth — and this is why we can always trust the Blockchain.

The ledger is simply a record and doesn't care whether a Bitcoin represents a certain amount of Euros or Dollars, or anything else of value, or property for that matter. Users can decide for themselves what a unit of Bitcoin represents. A Bitcoin is divisible in a hundred million units and each unit is both individually identifiable and programmable. This means that users can assign properties to each unit. Users can programme a unit to represent a Euro Cent, or a share in a company, a kilowatt hour of energy, or a digital Certificate of Ownership. Because of this, Bitcoin is much more than simply money and payments. A Bitcoin can represent many kinds of property: a thousand barrels of oil, award credits, or a vote during elections, for example. Moreover, Bitcoin allows us to make our currency smarter and to automise our cash and money flows.

Imagine a healthcare allowance in Dollars or Euros that can only be used to pay for healthcare at certified parties. In this case, whether someone actually follows the rules is no longer verified in the bureaucratic process afterwards. You simply programme these rules into the money. The result of this is a whole lot less paperwork, and compliance up front when it comes to users. The unit can even be programmed in such a way that it will automatically return to the provider if the receiver doesn't use it after a certain amount of time. This way the provider can ensure the allowances are not hoarded.

A company can control its spending in the same way

by programming budgets for salaries, machinery, materials and maintenance so that the respective money is specified and cannot be spent on other things. Automating such matters leads to a considerable decrease in bureaucracy which saves accountants, controllers and the organisation in general an incredible amount of time. The programmable open character of Bitcoin allows us to completely rebuild and innovate our financial sector and our administrative processes, make them more efficient and transparent, and significantly decrease bureaucracy.

But there's more.

In an internet of things, our economy will be dealing with machines that actively participate in the economic traffic. In fact they're already here. Think of a vending machine or drones delivering packages. These machines are unfamiliar with the concept of trust, but Bitcoin is not. Because of Bitcoin the drone can be 100% certain that it will deliver the package to the right recipient and know for sure that it's been paid for, and we can programme the vending machine in such a way that it will automatically keep track of its supplies, order new supplies from the supplier, and pay for them automatically. Of course you'll understand that this is only the beginning.

Internet technology is disruptive and breaks the *status quo*. It opens markets and breaks the positions of middle men all the time.

Bitcoin and cryptocurrencies have caused a paradigm shift. It's time to explore this new technology constructively and critically, and openly discuss potential applications.

The Power of Distributed Networks

A centralised model, typical of central banking relies on a single server or group of servers. There is a single point of failure — vulnerable to attack.

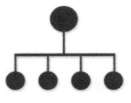

CENTRALISED

A distributed model is less vulnerable to attack but can suffer from inconsistency. At any one time, we cannot be certain that all nodes have access to the whole picture. There can be no true consensus

DECENTRALISED

A decentralised model is by nature distributed but has no central authority, nor a single point of failure.

DISTRIBUTED
NETWORK

PEER-TO-PEER

A blockchain however uses a distributed peer-to-peer model that provides a shared consensus – each node contains a full copy of the blockchain, updated every time another block is added – approximately every 10 minutes in the case of Bitcoin. Blockchain incorporates all the benefits of the previous models and uses peer to peer.

This achieves Distributed Consensus

In traditional models we require a trusted third party to execute transactions on our behalf. - "the bank" in the vast majority of cases

The consensus provided by the Blockchain does away with the necessity for this third party guarantor.

Blockchain itself is the guarantee.

And everyone in the network has access to the ledger, so it is completely transparent at all times.

But how does it work exactly?

All Bitcoin transactions are broadcast to each node on the network. They are collected together into 'blocks' then bound together into a 'chain' using strong cryptography. Thus it's called a blockchain because it is a chain of blocks. Miners compete to publish a block and add it to the chain and take the reward — currently 6.25 BTC or around $75,000

We now need to delve a little deeper and look at definitions and terms that are used in respect of the blockchain.

Miner

A special node, usually a computer or device which collects transactions from the transaction pool into blocks then verifies them. Can also refer to the owner of these devices

Each node takes the broadcasted transactions, forms them into a block and verifies which transactions are in fact valid. Although the purpose of the mining computers is to do the accounting for the block chain, most of the work they actually do is to add a nonce and generate the hash of the block.

Hash

Also called a message digest, is a number generated from a string of text. The hash is substantially smaller than the text itself, and is generated by a formula in such a way that it is astronomically unlikely — 1 in 10 to the power of 60 — which is a 10 followed by 60 zeroes— that some other text will produce the same hash value. To make the numbers involved here slightly more manageable they are written in base 16 — which uses the numbers 0 to 9 with a, b, c, d, e and f to create a 64 digit number. This is an example of a hash, just to show you what one looks like:

43919d1d79dd32f181433e668bc457cd016f62b6f20adb811 4d1c3b93954e1d3

Nonce

A nonce is a field in a Bitcoin block the value of which is randomly set by the node so that the hash of the block will contain a run of leading zeros. The word 'nonce' is an abbreviation of the term 'number appearing only once', and many nonce values are tried and the hash is recomputed until the hash contains the required number of leading zeros.

But how does that work exactly?

This is called Proof-of-Work — a costly operation which requires a lot of computer power and hence electricity to carry it out, via a one way function, sometimes known as a 'trapdoor' function.

Bitcoin could actually operate perfectly well without Proof-of-Work, as long as everyone was perfectly honest and altruistic. If they are not, then reaching a consensus is difficult. We need the miners to compete, and we in fact need them not to trust each other. The greed of the miners competing to find a solution gives us a mechanism that all can trust. Then, the first miner to find a valid solution that meets the standard of difficulty, puts their signature on the block, adds it to the chain, and the process starts again approximately every 10 minutes

Because a significant number of people have agreed the solution, it is valid.

This is called Distributed Consensus.

How blocks are linked

Within a blockchain, each block is linked to the block

behind it by that block's digital signature. Each block consists of the accumulated transactions that have occurred since the last block was broadcast; a timestamp; the key of the miner who completed that block; and the hash or signature of the previous block. Once updated, the ledger cannot be altered or tampered with. This is because there is effectively a one way door out of the block but no way back in.

New blocks are broadcast to everyone in the network at the same time.

The fact that future blocks rely on the signatures of those that have gone before, makes it impossible to generate your own string of blocks to attack the network. If you wanted to impose your own version of reality — such as: "Yes I really did pay him 120 BTC last Tuesday", you would need to control more than 50% of the network.

This emphasises the importance of having a large number of nodes, none of whom trust each other, because they are all competing for the reward of being first to complete the block and earn the Bitcoins.

How do we know it's secure?

The first point to remember is that all the information is sent to every participant in the system immediately it happens.

On top of that, multiple copies make it much harder to hack — the distributed nature of a blockchain database means that it's harder for anyone to attack it . Remember that each node holds a complete copy of the blockchain.

Hackers would have to access every copy of the database and change each one simultaneously to be successful.

Another level of security involves comparing the cryptographic hashes, which would show if there are any anomalies. This concept can be extended to ensure that any file or digital asset we receive is what we expected by comparing the cryptographic hashes. It also keeps every piece of data secure and private because the hash cannot be converted back into the original data — it's a one-way process. So, if the original document or transaction, or in fact any piece of the data within a block were subsequently altered, it would produce a totally different digital signature, alerting the network to the mismatch. The result of this is that mismatches are immediately obvious. If the original document or transaction were ever altered by even one bit, it would produce a completely different digital signature.

OTHER USES OF BLOCKCHAIN TECHNOLOGY

So far, we have looked at how blokchain technology has been implemented to create the currency known as Bitcoin.

Bitcoin began as a person-to-person electronic cash system. Anyone can hold Bitcoin and pay anyone else without a trusted third-party, or middle-man. Bitcoin is the most widely known application of blockchain technology and serves its purpose as a digital currency extremely effectively — to date there has never been an instance of the system either failing, or being hacked, and it is likely to stay this way.

Despite this however, Bitcoin should not be seen as the perfect implementation of blockchain technology. Issues exist with Bitcoin such as scaling, blockchain size, and the fact that Proof-of-Work mining is extremely energy wasteful. It is estimated that the current total energy expended on Proof-of-Work is equal to that used by Cambodia — think about that for a minute — an entire country! But as time has gone on, more and more 'mining' is being powered by renewable energy. It probably is presently more than 50% of all Bitcoin mining energy.

There are other considerations concerning the effectivness of Bitcoin, such as lack of true privacy due to the public nature of the ledger. It is in fact possible to mine Bitcoin transaction metadata, and some contemporary cryptocurrencies such as Dash and Zcash attempt to address this.

Absolute anonymity is a double-edged sword as far as governments are concerned, and because there is often a need for this in carrying out financial transactions, we will begin to see private or permissioned currencies begin to be developed.

Other currencies have been developed on a variety of themes, and linked to a variety of services. Uniswap is a coin that is linked to a major cryptocurrency exchange; Chainlink is a currency which is linked to the use of smart contracts, written into a blockchain; and there are cryptocurrencies too, linked to geographical groups and cultures. Scotcoin is one such of these, and aims to be a national cryptocurrency, intended as a way for Scots to transact with each other and all who wish to trade with Scotland. To make this a reality, a cryptocurrency like Scotcoin will need to operate on what is known as a 'permissioned blockchain'. That is to say, formal verification of identity will be required before an account to operate on the Scotcoin blockchain will be issued to a person wishing to use the currency.

*

Multiple Uses and Global Reach

Any person can use cryptocurrencies to send money around the world. This is especially important for nations such as the Philippines where a significant percentage of GDP is derived from remittances by its citizens working abroad. As well as payments and transfers, cryptocurrencies can be ideal for microtransactions, such as tipping, collecting donations and crowdfunding. This is because of low transaction costs, and because there might not be a need in these circumstances for payments to be absolutely immediate.

Payment Infrastructure

Merchants can accept cryptocurrency payments. This is slightly different than using a cryptocurrency like Bitcoin as a currency. There are in fact merchant processing and remittance services, such as BitPay and Abra.

Merchants and businesses accepting credit card payments or other point-of-sale processing will often pay a fixed fee and a percentage of the transaction to the processor. Bitcoin requires only the network to be paid to confirm the transaction, and the mining fee is paid by the sender, not the receiver. Fees are much lower on a like-for-like basis and scale well for large values.

Digital Assets

A blockchain can be used to create digital assets such as stocks, bonds, land titles, and frequent-flyer miles. These assets are created using protocols on top of the Bitcoin Blockchain. Examples include Coloredcoins.

We can use permissioned as well as private blockchains to control how users are able to interact with the blockchain. By using KYC (Know Your Customer) or AML (Anti Money Laundering) procedures we can restrict access to approved users only.

In the world of buying and selling stocks and shares, there is effectively an eighteenth century system in place. There are at least three lots of people who have to deal with the buying and selling of stocks. The broker, the market maker, the registrar all create bits of paper that have to be passed backwards and forwards. It can take a fortnight and more to get a share certificate. If shares are traded on a blockchain, it is as simple as one person sending another person some cryptocurrency. The blockchain would say that I owned stock in MegaCorp Inc. — and you would hand me some money. I would transfer the stock by inputting your digital ID onto the blockchain, and hey presto! You would own the stock and I would have the cash. That's why on the blockchain, the trade is the settlement — or the settlement is the trade. Either way, it's virtually instantaneous. And the Bitcoin Blockchain can also be used as a trusted timestamp for arbitrary messages just as well as it can be used for anything that is time critical.

Companies using this technology in such a manner include Chain, NASDAQ, Openchain and Overstock, which uses its own tZERO protocol.

Identity

Blockchain technology can be used to store and provide publicly verifiable proof of identity. For example, a company providing traditional KYC and AML checks could publish and sign a transaction on a blockchain to say that the individual has provided proof of their identity. Companies already providing these services include Onename, Blockstack and Keybase.

This idea can be enhanced by providing a user-controlled front-end to the process by which the user themselves determines what details can be made visible, if any. One such implementation of this idea is miiCard. The idea is that services like this allow the user direct control over their data.

Secure and unique identity management has ramifications for a vast number of applications including access to government services like our NHS and can be deployed in such a way to provide provably fair and highly tamper-resistant voting for a variety of end purposes.

Smart contracts

Smart contracts are computer protocols that facilitate, verify, or enforce the negotiation or performance of a contract, or make a contractual clause unnecessary.

Smart contracts can be implemented in a distributed ledger as well as a non-distributed ledger system.

Blockchains are one type of such distributed ledger system that, when sufficiently secured, make it impossible for a single party or group of parties to reverse transactions once recorded on this database. This eliminates the need for trusted intermediaries to authenticate and settle transactions. As we have seen earlier, effectively there is a notary present at every transaction.

As a result of these properties, smart contracts on distributed ledgers could have a high degree of immutability and security, guaranteeing execution based on coded terms.

Digital Autonomous Organisations

Digital Autonomous Organisations are organisations or corporate entities that are run through rules encoded as computer programs called smart contracts. A DAO's financial transaction record and program rules — that is to say, its business operating methods — are maintained on a blockchain. Such organisations are therefore not tied to any particular nation state, meaning that the precise legal status of this type of business organisation is unclear at this time.

Several examples exist of this type of business model. For instance, consider a fleet of electric driverless taxis. Passengers would call a taxi and agree a fare. Each taxi would have its own cryptocurrency wallet to collect fares, pay for recharging and maintenance, cleaning and all other business costs. Before accepting any hire the taxi would check it had sufficient range to complete the hire and whether any maintenance was required. Low oil, worn tyres? Head instead to the nearest smart-contracted maintenance facility. If not, take passengers to destination and collect fare on arrival. All taxes, congestion charges and other administrative fucntions would be settled by smart contract. At the end of its useful life , the car could even drive itself to the scrap yard.

This is a fairly simple example. Far more complex models are already being planned and others will become possible as the technology improves and more human ingenuity is applied.

Many of these new initiatives have serious implications for employment and society will have to be ready to adapt to fast and comprehensive structural changes.

It has often been said that robots will change our lives. For some time now we have had the hardware. With the introduction of AI (Artificial Intelligence) and blockchain technology to oversee and regulate these robots, that day is fast approaching.

WHAT NEXT FOR DIGITAL CURRENCY?

Not all cryptocurrencies are mined. Some are what are called pre-mined. In other words, from day one the decision has been taken that only a specific number of coins or tokens will be created. There are four main methods of creating consensus and many different types of cryptocurrencies, as well as uses for them.

The Bitcoin Bockchain uses Proof-of-work as a way of mining coins, and this is inherently very wasteful of resources, using massive amounts of power. Ethereum in its second incarantion, ETH 2.0 uses a Proof-of-Stake method of consensus, which is much less wasteful.

Block time

Perhaps one of the most important reasons why so many other cryptocurrencies — called 'alt coins' — have proliferated, is because the number of transactions that can be done on the Bitcoin blockchain, and the length of time it takes to do them.

With Bitcoin, a new block is created roughly every 10 minutes. In other words the absolute fastest a transaction can be confirmed is every 10 minutes. Align that with the fact that only some seven or eight transactions can be effected every second, and you have some pretty hefty reasons to do something different. Litecoin for example was an attempt to speed up transactions. Litecoin aimed to handle transactions at a speed of around fifty-six per second, although in practice it has not managed to achieve this. Ethereum 2.0 aims to conduct around 10,000 transactions per second

Community

Digital currency aficionados like to refer to themselves as being in an Ecosystem. All it really means is that a number of people and businesses have come together and have all agreed to accept and trade a particular currency. A very good example of this is the currency known as Kin, which is the currency used by the Kik messaging App. It is worth looking at this in some depth.

What Is Kin?

As with many other company-specific digital currencies, Kin has special uses within the Kik messenger platform. Users are able to earn Kin for making contributions to the broader Kik community; and they can also spend Kin on various goods and services within the Kik platform

Kin was first launched in September of 2017. It was launched via an ICO that raised roughly $100 million in investor funds over a period of about two weeks. Upon its launch, the founders of Kin described the Kin Ecosystem as "designed specifically to bring people together in a new shared economy," with the cryptocurrency itself acting as a "foundation for a decentralised ecosystem of digital services."

While most companies that launch their own cryptocurrency have a ready-made user base, Kik had an important advantage over its competitors in this regard. Kik already enjoyed millions of active users through its messaging platform. As such, the platform could drive mainstream consumer adoption of the Kin cryptocurrency. The Kik app was also able to house many of the traditionally third-party services and features for the currency, including the Kin wallet.

Kin Rewards Engine

Perhaps one of the most promising and exciting aspect of the launch of Kin has been the Kin Rewards Engine. Through this mechanism, "Kin will be introduced into circulation as a daily reward, to be distributed among stakeholders by an algorithm that reflects each community's contribution to the overall ecosystem."

This is one of many ways that the makers of Kin have worked to incentivise the use of the cryptocurrency by the broader Kik community. Apps are still able to offer Kin to consumers in exchange for watching advertisements and providing feedback, as most cryptocurrencies operating in a similar fashion already do.

Besides this, though, consumers are able to engage in

a much wider variety of activities in exchange for Kin tokens. The Kin development team assumes that consumers don't enjoy having to watch ads in order to be rewarded in cryptocurrency, no matter how much they might like the reward. For that reason, it's possible for Kik users to amass Kin tokens without ever having to watch advertisements.

Kik CEO and founder Ted Livingston has suggested that the Kin token is an opportunity to distribute value amongst developers. The idea is that Kik will give away value, incentivising developers to "build an open and decentralized ecosystem of apps" on the Kik platform.

The Kin Foundation is a "manifestation of a not-for-profit governance organization that will ultimately be decentralized and autonomous," helping to steer the development of the broader ecosystem, according to ETHnews (quoted in Investopedia Jun 25th 2019). The ecosystem will not be based around advertising, as many social media platforms are, but rather on users being able to provide value to themselves and one another, and on those users then being rewarded for that contribution.

Besides being a digital currency, the Kin website describes the token as "different from other digital currencies because it is a cryptocurrency." Kin is similar to Bitcoin in that it makes use of the public blockchain and has monetary value. The fact that Kin is part of a blockchain allows its developers to control the creation and flow of tokens to prevent a surge. Blockchain support also allows a token to be guaranteed over the long term.

While many cryptocurrencies reward powerful mining operations and encourage users to stockpile tokens, Kin's setup prompts Kik users to earn and spend their currency within the platform. Kin is seamlessly integrated into apps, with Kin-supported apps in the Kik platform set apart with a small "K" icon. Those icons link apps with the Kin Marketplace, where users can find many different opportunities to both earn and spend their tokens.

This is also the hub where developers are able to create and distribute content for Kin rewards. In these ways, Kik's developers have worked to integrate the cryptocurrency into the app experience, assuring that customers do not have to go out of their way in order to become involved in the Kin economy.

If Facebook were to consider doing such a thing with their own cryptocurrency, their global reach is such that they would be in a position to virtually offer humanity its first form of UBI (Universal Basic Income). We could in fact be paid for sharing our data with them, bceause we are all creating data, and all the time, like it our not.

Where to buy my digital currency?

Coinbase: Coinbase is the world's largest Bitcoin (BTC) broker. They represent an easy and fast way for new users to purchase bitcoins, ethereum, litecoin and many other coins.

Poliniex: Poloniex used to be the largest cryptocurrency exchange, but lost many of its users when it had trouble scaling to support a surge of new signups. Recently, Poloniex was acquired by Circle, which is partly backed by Goldman Sachs, one of the largest investment banks in the US.

Binance: Binance is a cryptocurrency exchange based in Malta — or somewhere. No one is very sure, which has led to various regulatory problems recently. It remains the largest by a long way. It has very low fees at just 0.05% per trade. Once you purchase Litecoin, Bitcoin or Ethereum you can use Binance to convert one of those three coins into nearly any altcoin.

Luno: Luno is a Bitcoin exchange based in Singapore. It originally launched to support countries like South Africa and Indonesia, but recently expanded to Europe and supports the purchase of Bitcoin through credit, SEPA transfer, SOFORT and iDEAL

There are many more exchanges available, worldwide

Where to spend my digital currency?

Many large companies are accepting Bitcoin as a legitimate source of funds. You can spend your Bitcoin at major companies such as Microsoft, Expedia, Wikipedia and Amazon (by using purse.io).

SECURITY

One of the facts about Blockchain technology is that it insists we take responsibility for our own security.

For this chapter we turn to cryptocurrency and security expert Danette Wallace, and an article titled *Blockchain Will Force Us To Put Our Big Boy / Big Girl Pants On*.

Danette titled her article this way because of the fact that when we transition to digital currencies and blockchain applications, we will need to collectively grow up.

In western culture, we are accustomed to depending on external organisations to take care of our assets. Banks take care of our money; trusts take care of our properties; stock brokers take care of our investments. If we have an issue in any of these areas, there is a backup system in place. These external organisations are responsible for backing up our information because essentially we don't own the data — they do.

The irony is that there is a sense of freedom that comes when your information is captured — much like there is a sense of freedom for children who don't have to worry about paying for rent or food because their parents take care of it. As a society, we're like children. We're free of the worry of being 100% responsible for our information because centralised organisations take care of it. The problem is, however, that they also own it. With blockchain, all of that will change.

A shift of responsibility

With the move to digital currencies and blockchain applications, the safety of our assets and our sensitive information will become our individual responsibility. Currently, this is not the case. If we lose a valuable document, we can recover it from the organisation that is responsible for keeping a record of it. There is often a record of what we own somewhere in the bureaucratic universe.

Because of this backup system, our minds tend to think of digital assets as 'copies' of something that exists in the cloud somewhere. With decentralised blockchains, however, the original data exists on individual nodes only. In other words, the original data will often exist only in our phones. That's what makes blockchain so different from other technologies. It allows for the digital asset to be the 'original,' just like cash. But also like cash, if you lose it — you lose it.

Time to grow up

This may be a difficult transition for some. We all have that friend who seems to misplace their keys every other week or the family member who can't find their eyeglasses even when the glasses are sitting on top of their head. These are the individuals who may have the hardest time with this new responsibility.

A number of people have lost millions of dollars worth of Bitcoin from being careless with their personal passwords to their Bitcoin accounts. Since the password doesn't exist on a central database, if the person loses their password, there's no way to recover it and the Bitcoin sits on the blockchain with no way to access it. Of the existing 18.5 million Bitcoin mined by 2021, around 20 percent — currently worth around $140 billion — appear to be in lost or otherwise stranded wallets, according to the cryptocurrency data firm Chainalysis. These coins are left inaccessible and permanently lost on the Bitcoin blockchain. If you don't want to lose access to your cryptocurrency, do whatever you can to keep your passwords safe.

Andreas Antonopoulos, one of the foremost Bitcoin experts, prints out his passwords and key phrases and puts the paper copies in bank safety deposit boxes. This is ironic given that Antonopoulos thinks banks will go by the wayside when cryptocurrency enters mainstream. I tend to agree with him. I have always said that banks should consider transitioning from monetary banks to information banks. That way they will continue to remain relevant.

Do your homework and know who and what to trust

With the transition to blockchain, we will need to shift our trust from the banking system and government organisations to trusting the blockchain protocol. Blockchain is a unique technology because it's able to hold records of people's assets in a decentralised framework. Blockchain is often referred to as a trust-less system which means, that with blockchain, we don't need to trust people or institutions. The trust resides in the technology itself.

For some, trusting blockchain protocols may be difficult at first. This is often due to their misunderstanding of where to appropriately place their trust. The trust-less aspect of a blockchain comes into play when the technology is used as it was intended…as a decentralised consensus platform. Trust should not be placed in centralised databases, even if they say they are using a blockchain. If such organisations are using a centralised blockchain, then they are not using blockchain as it was intended. The user should be mature in their pursuit of knowledge and in their decision making and they should know who to trust.

For example, those that have done their homework know that the Bitcoin protocol has proven its trustworthiness. In the twelve years that Bitcoin has been around, there has not been a successful theft from the protocol yet. This does not mean that people don't try. Hackers are constantly trying to hack into Bitcoin. The reason they're unsuccessful is because of the decentralised nature of the protocol. To successfully compromise the system, a hacker would need to gain consensus from the community to implement their changes but hackers are never able to gain that consensus. This is why a decentralised blockchain is safer than a centralised one.

Regulations and laws do not prevent hackers from hacking into Bitcoin — the decentralised community does.

When data is kept in a centralised exchange, it's more susceptible to theft and corruption. This is why it's important to first — know the difference between a centralised blockchain and a decentralised blockchain and then — to put our trust in the appropriate decentralised blockchains.

For proof of the safety of decentralised frameworks, all you have to do is look at the evidence.

• Amount of Bitcoin stolen from the decentralised Bitcoin protocol — $0

• Amount of Bitcoin stolen from centralised exchanges — $15 Billion

When there is a shift in trust from centralised organisations to decentralised blockchains and we gain an aptitude to know the difference, we will take on a new responsibility for the safety of our assets. That's when we will collectively grow from blockchain infants to blockchain adolescents and have our big boy / big girl pants on.

DICTIONARY OF TERMS

One of the most baffling aspects of blockchain technology and cryptocurrency, is the jargon. New ideas need new languages, and the language of crypto is no exception.

In reading the following list you'll see some terms in particular that refer to what is known as Public Key Cryptography, — also known as asymmetric cryptography. This is any cryptographic system that uses pairs of keys — somewhat similar to a bank safety deposit box where your private key is needed as well as the bank's own key.

In the cryptographic system we have public keys — which may be disseminated widely, and private keys which are known only to the owner. This accomplishes two functions: authentication, which is when the public key is used to verify that a holder of the paired private key sent the message; and encryption, whereby only the holder of the paired private key can decrypt the message encrypted with the public key.

Security then depends only on keeping the private key private, and the public key may be published without compromising security.

Altcoin

Any cryptocurrency other than Bitcoin; literally an 'alternative coin.'

Bitcoin

The original and most prominent example of a cryptocurrency.

Blockchain

The underlying technology that are the foundation for cryptocurrencies.

Cryptocurrency

A digital currency in which public key encryption techniques are used to verify the transfer of funds and regulate the generation of units of currency.

Cryptocurrency Exchanges

Platforms that allow users to buy, sell or trade cryptocurrency.

Cryptography

A method used to encrypt, or scramble, the contents of a file in such a way that only those with the knowledge of how to decrypt, or unscramble, the contents can read it.

Hash

Also called a message digest, a hash is a number generated from a string of text. The hash is substantially smaller than the text itself, and is generated by a formula in such a way that it is astronomically unlikely (1 in 10 to the power of 60) that some other text will produce the same hash value.

Hashpower

Hashpower, also known as the"hash rate", is the speed at which transactions are verified on the blockchain.

Miner

A special node, usually a computer or device which collects transactions from the transaction pool into blocks then verifies them.

Mining

The process of verifying transactions on the block-chain. With Bitcoin, mining is the process by which new bitcoins are brought into circulation, but it is also a key component of the maintenance and development of the blockchain ledger. Mining is performed usually using specially designed computers that solve highly complex computational problems.

Node

A site connected to the blockchain network holding a copy of the blockchain

Nonce

A field in a Bitcoin block whose value is randomly set by the node so that the hash of the block will contain a run of leading zeros. Many nonce values are tried and the hash is recomputed until the hash contains the required number of leading zeros.

Private Key

A long number (32 bytes) generated using a complex mathematical formula

Proof of Stake

Is the framework in which a user's stake determines how much say they have in verifying each blockchain

Proof of Work

Is the process by which miners are rewarded for their work to verify the blockchain.

Public Key

A cryptographic key that can be obtained and used by

anyone to encrypt messages intended for a particular recipient, such that the encrypted messages can be deciphered only by using a second key that is known only to the recipient (the private key).

P2P (Peer-to-peer)

Is the process of passing information directly from one computer (peer) to another, without needing to pass through a central location

Tokens

Are used to transfer or pay through cryptocurrency, and represent just about any asset that has worth and can be traded.

Wallet

A graphical software program that manages private keys and generates public keys (addresses) and can interact with the blockchain.

RESOURCES

Where to buy my digital currency?

There are many online exchanges across the world now that will sell digital currency. All of them require that customers go through KYC (Kn ow Your Customer) and AML (Anti Money Laundering) procedures. ALWAYS write down your passphrases and store them in a safe place. I advocate taking a photograph AND writing them down in two separate, different places. Remember, lose that phrase and the wallet and all it contains is lost

Where to spend my digital currency?

This is becoming easier, as more and more places accept digital currency. Remember crypto currencies are a store of and a method of transferring value

How to keep my digital currency safe?

You should store your coins offline with only relatively small quantities for immediate access. Think of offline as a deposit account and online as your current account

CONCLUSION

I hope this guide has helped you understand what Blockchain technology is all about, and what its relationship is with Bitcoin and other crypto and digital currencies. There are several appendices attached which illustrateand show the further development of Blockchain and amplify some other issues.

What does the future hold?

If you are a believer, like me, you will probably feel that the way we record data and how we use it will change completely, once again.

One of the more interesting things to note is that we are steadily moving up the blockchain ladder. If the Bitcoin blockchain was Generation 1, then Hyperledger was Generation 2. We are now on Generation 3, which encompasses, for example, Facebook's Libra, and which is known as a Permissioned Decentralised Blockchain, because it maintains an access control layer which allows certain actions to be performed only by certain identifiable participants. For these reason, these blockchains differ from public and private blockchains.

Whereas Hyperledger is a stack or suite of programs, largely being checked and managed by IBM, the third generation are using open source blockchains to create what is called Blockchain as a Service (BaaS for short) platforms. These operate at a fraction of the cost and working hours required to bring them to full capability. In general terms a BaaS installation will be around 7-10% of the full Hyperledger stack.

There are very good reasons to use a blockchain solution in many industries. Take a look at Appendix 1 for the questions you need to ask to find out if Blockchain is for you.

It is important you remember that it isn't necessary to absolutely, utterly and completely understand the Blockchain. Much like mobile phones, you don't need to know how they work – as long as you can make a phone call. The same applies to Blockchain. You don't need to know *all* the intricacies; rather just enough to understand that it is safe, secure, easy to use and groundbreaking.

There are other considerations. Bitcoin's blockchain is validated using Proof of Work consensus (see Appendix 2) Proof of Work is inherently wasteful of The Earth's resources. It is estimated that Bitcoin uses 150,000,000 Megawatts of Electricity a year. That's more than Holland and Belgium put together. In the long run this is a serious drag on Bitcoin's expansion, not only from a cost perspective but from a Green and Eco-friendly point of view. The newer generations of blockchains use other forms of validation (Proof of Stake, Kafka, PoET etc – see Appendix 2) These are all much more sustainable – Proof of Stake in particular would mean using only the power for a dozen tumble driers to power Bitcoin.

Bitcoin itself has staged a remarkable recovery. From a low of about $3150, it has been as high as $65,000, before dropping to below $30,000, and heading back up. Predictions of as high as $300,000 abound this year, but I don't think anyone would take bets on the year end price at the moment. Traditionally, Bitcoin has tended to fall back towards the end of the year, but then establish a lower plateau in the first quarter of the following year, and a further advance at the end of Quarter 2 and during Quarter 3.

What we have been through is known as "The Hype Cycle".

You can see that this translates into how new technologies are adopted. You only have to think of the Tech Revolution of the early 2000s where the landscape was literally strewn with failed businesses. But some of those businesses have in fact burgeoned. Amazon, EBay and Netflix were all incorporated mid to late 1990s, suffered mightily from the early 2000s fall-out, but have gone on to become the behemoths of their time.

Blockchain is as we speak at the level of the second wave of media hype. I believe this time round it will progress to encompass all the industries I have mentioned.

I had a most interesting conversation the other day with what in the past would have been called " The Man on the Clapham Omnibus." This man claimed never to have heard of Bitcoin – and hence had never heard of the blockchain. I asked him if he was on Facebook, and he replied that he was. I then asked him if he had heard of

Facebook's digital currency, Libra - now changed and called Diem. "Oh yes," he said "I know all about that!" And he really did. The point here is that perhaps 50-80 million people were aware of Bitcoin and blockchain in April 2019. By July, 2.7 billion people knew what a crypto/digital currency was. That is a step change which alone will have significant and far-reaching consequences.

It has been over 20 years since Bill Gates opined: "Banking is essential, banks are not." This is now so obvious as to be almost a given, and is one of the reasons that so many of the banks with their enormously expensive legacy systems have been so against Bitcoin. Interestingly, they are very much less against blockchain itself. In fact, most of them are already working with different consultants to come up with a way to make use of blockchain, and in consequence to reduce their costs. That has to be their focus and is part of the reason for branch closures and the move to a cashless society. It won't happen overnight; there will be a lot of kicking and screaming along the way, and there will always be some cash floating about, but it will happen.

A couple of years ago the Royal mint in the UK didn't make any 20pence or £2 coins. Why? Because there were already more sloshing around the system than there was a use for. Businesses are already moving cashless; Domino's Pizza recently as well as ITSU spring to mind;, and there are seriously attractive reasonsfor businesses to do this.

Typically, what happens in a venue that takes cash?

First thing in the morning you have to check the float. Do you need more change? Nip to the bank where they will charge you 80p per £100. You give and take change all day and (horrors) when you cash up at night it's short! Then you have to take the money back to the bank where they charge you another 80p per £100. And none of that includes the cost of time and the poor person who has to count it all.

So commercially speaking, not taking cash saves quite decent sums of money, as well as a lot of time and working hours. In businesses that go down this route, quite a number are giving themselves a better commercial advantage by lowering their prices. Making full use of contactless (which by the way means there is never a cash shortfall and there is a proper record of every transaction) also means that it is not a step so far to taking digital currencies as well. Oh, and there's one other benefit. Your insurance premium goes down too. No cash, much lower premium. No cash overnight, much lower premium again. And you don't have to be insured to take cash to the bank either.

What are digital currencies advantages over fiat money – by which we mean the money we use every day like British Pounds or US Dollars?

Firstly, the transaction cost is infinitesimal compared to fiat transfers. Sending £1million to Africa from the UK will cost between £20 and 30,000. Doing the same thing with cryptocurrencies would be £1-2. Yes there are other considerations, but that alone is a powerful argument for making it work. Indeed, this is the very thing that Ripple (Token name:XRP) seeks to address, and several banks are in fact involved with this.

The second advantage is more nuanced. You can target the crypto. For example, if you only want people selling baby clothes to receive the crypto, once the sellers are registered it is child's play to enable any crypto to only be exchangeable at those outlets. That, of course, can be applied to any industry, charity, project or person.

So what of the future? The Age of Bitcoin only started with Nakamoto's White Paper in 2009 so in financial terms it's not even an infant. It's hardly surprising, therefore, that there are lots of Alarums and Excursions along the way.

But consider this. The first Cryptocurrency was not Bitcoin when it was first mined in 2010.

It was a thing called WIR, created in the 1930s in Switzerland (see Page XX). In essence, that was a period when there was no liquidity in any financial markets. To survive this period, the good Burghers of Zurich decided they need some form of token to trade between themselves. And so WIR was born. This currency has remained almost unchanged to this day; some CHF 6.5 billion of trade is done annually with it, 70,000 businesses accept it and over 550,000 Swiss also use it. The real point – and one worth labouring – is you don't have to just use WIR. You can pay for something in Switzerland using half WIR, half Swiss Franc; or any combination of the two you like.

What the Blockchain could mean?

Over the last few years there has been much discussion and controversy about Bitcoin, but in more recent times there has been an even greater interest in the technology underpinning this digital currency. The platform, or rather the protocol, known as the Blockchain is now widely acknowledged as having profound consequences for the worlds of finance, supply chains, logistics, and the Internet of Things.

Ethereum and the next stage of blockchain

As the technology permits robust financial transactions at a time when companies face significant challenges in data management and security, hundreds of companies are looking to use Blockchain to make and verify transactions without reference to a central authority, or are experimenting with distributed ledger technology as a secure and transparent way to digitally track the ownership of assets.

Bitcoin has, to put it mildly, acquired a mixed reputation. Yet, The Bank of England has described it as a significant key innovation for society and finance in general and many companies have already created applications and uses to be built upon the Blockchain that would really make things revolutionary.

For example, Ethereum allows the creation of so-called 'smart contracts'. Whilst the Blockchain allows currencies such as Bitcoin to use a specific scripting language for transactions, Ethereum uses a more complex language, and allows users to program into any digital transaction certain conditions, rights, permissions and / or restrictions before or after it allows a transaction to occur. To this extent, these are not exactly ' contracts' and I personally prefer using the term 'smart permissions'.

Using 'Ether tokens' to ensure that programmed tasks

and restrictions have been fulfilled allows for a wider use of the technology beyond creation a cryptocurrency, and this includes decentralised data storage, decentralised voting, shared savings accounts and many asset management tasks.

Theoretically, Ethereum can be programmed to serve almost any purpose including the dissemination of any information. With this significant level of flexibility, many foresee this as the most powerful and impactful new digital platform since the creation of the internet and the worldwide web.

What are the applications for Blockchain outside of finance/data transactions?

There are now hundreds of startups in the Blockchain space, with hundreds more companies and firms within commerce and banking creating, incubating and acquiring companies in this area.

In October 2018, The Economist's front page "How the technology behind Bitcoin could change the world" caught many business leaders' imaginations and the newspaper identified that as the moment when Blockchain companies were currently fulfilling tasks in three broad areas:

1. Asset transfers: Using Blockchain's ability to transfer digital assets or create data to attach to 'real world' transfers/transactions.

2. A truth machine: Blockchain transactions being

combined with key information which can and will be forever embedded in the ledger, such as the provenance of a piece of art or a gem providing unchallengeable evidence in the case of theft.

3. Smart contracts (or smart permissions): Allowing transactions on the Blockchain to be programmed to execute subject to the fulfilment of certain conditions.

The opportunity for the Blockchain is that it could represent the 'internet of value'. By being, in and of itself, a robust payment platform it could allow rights owners to remove brokers and other payment providers that deduct anything between 1% to 30% simply for 'reselling' goods in an online environment.

Selling digital goods is complex and not nearly as 'cost free' as many people may assume. With the cost of handling chargebacks, fraud prevention and security systems being so high, the Blockchain could enable robust secure transactions without these extra costs, and ease business to consumer sales.

The use of smart contracts (or smart permissions) provides the opportunity to bind payments and transaction to certain actions and outcomes. Whilst smart contracts will not dispose of the need for contracts and/or lawyers (smart or otherwise), they could significantly reduce bureaucracy, paperwork and deliver memos that currently need to be put in place around the digitisation of virtually all content, whilst at the same time providing the opportunity to 'embed' non-invasive rights management technology into author permissions. By way of example, the Blockchain could enable an original music file to be stored along with a cryptographic hash detailing all the creators and rights holders, with percentages and revenue flows encoded into the file so that payments could be made on a near instantaneous basis. In the music industry, collecting societies are looking at Blockchain technology as a way of meeting their obligations to provide stakeholders with greater transparency. Information could be encoded into any online media asset in relation to chain of title and ownership, which could significantly ease the due diligence parties are currently required to undertake prior to the acquisition and/or exploitation of content.

I am now regularly asked by people whether or not the Blockchain could ever really be a 'thing', usually preceded by the question: "What is this Blockchain thingy?" My settled view is that the same disbelief greeted the World Wide Web, mobile technology, streaming, safe harbour platforms and the new world of embedded content and messaging, social media platforms and apps. Just as twenty years ago, the advent of the web allowed us to freely exchange information, the Blockchain allows us to freely exchange value. The fact that intellectual property rights do not 'sit comfortably' on these platforms does not appear to have been any impediment to whether or not these platforms eventually become 'a thing' (or indeed, everything).

Consider Napster. Napster demonstrated that customers wanted access to as much music as possible, quickly, and through peer-to-peer technology. Napster was of course shut down – but what it offered has since been developed and underpins many of the world's content management systems. To this extent, one could draw comparisons between Napster and Bitcoin and, consequently, between peer-to-peer and the Blockchain.

The only difference is that, unlike those other technologies that allowed for the free, unfettered, and uncontrolled use of content, the Blockchain might represent an opportunity to capture content and create value for its authors.

And that, everybody is what the future holds. An essentially cashless society using a combination of crypto and fiat currencies to transact its business. Safely and securely.

APPENDIX 1

Information on Scotcoin

Scotcoin is a digital currency in Scotland and beyond. Started by Derek Nisbet in 2013, Scotcoin languished after the Scottish Independence Referendum was lost in 2014. Beginning in 2015, David Low and Temple Melville, Glasgow businessmen, bought the IP and coin from Nisbet and proceeded to broaden and expand the depth and knowledge of the coin

Scotcoin is now one of the longest lived country crypto currencies. Scotcoin has moved to an ERC20 Ethereum Mainnet token, both verified by Etherscan and code audited with their highest rating by hacken.io. Scotcoin is in the process of moving to its own permissioned blockchain which encompasses KYC (Know Your Customer) and AML (Anti Money Laundering) to comply with all present and potential future regulations, as well as superior ERC protocols. There are several thousand holders of Scotcoin and the currency has holders in more than 50 countries worldwide. Scotcoin intends to occupy the social good works ecosystem and their plans are well advanced to do this.

Quite separately, The Scotcoin Project CIC is the charitable and educational arm of Scotcoin. Its task is to distribute Scotcoin to the people of Scotland; inform Scotland's people about their new digital currency; educate the public, businesses and agencies about Scotcoin, cryptocurrency and blockchain technologies. The Scotcoin Project will ensure Scotcoin is widely accepted in all areas of commerce and society in Scotland and beyond; incentivise and stimulate local trading initiatives; occupy the Charitable and Giving spaces and assist charities generally.

In addition, Scotcoin has a successful MeetUp group that meets bi-monthly around the country. A number of initiatives in the Charity Ecosector have already been undertaken, in particular with Social Bite, Eatup Charity , Bobath Scotland and others.

An advisory board is now in place which includes Ed Crozier, former president of the Scottish Rugby Union.

The number of holders of Scotcoin has increased from about 500 when the present management took over to around 3,500 now, and this number continues to grow. In addition, the very first property to be sold for crypto currency in Scotland was effected using Scotcoin in 2017

"A FLAT Glasgow's south side is the first property in the country to be bought with digital currency, rather than Sterling.

A Corby businessman, Peter McGowan, last week purchased the two-bedroom apartment in Bridge Street for 10 million Scotcoin, the equivalent of £60,000.

McGowan bought the flat from Glasgow businessman David Low, who owns Scotcoin's intellectual property

Both invested in Scotcoin shortly after the currency's launch in 2014.

"Peter wanted a flat and I wanted more Scotcoin," Low said of the sale, "so we're both happy."

Source: Glasgow Herald, 20th August 2017

Some time ago, Scotcoin realised that regulation would come to the crypto world, and so the Project have been working to produce a new blockchain onto which the existing coin can be migrated. To comply with laws that will shortly be enacted, this blockchain will be KYC and AML compliant.

The new ERC20 coin is now in existence and available for existing holders to migrate to, and new members to buy. The five founding principles for the new blockchain are:

1. An efficient and cost effective migration process,

2. A robust blockchain solution,

3. Un-issued surplus coin creation (for reward and future distribution),

4. Access to an efficient secondary market or markets and

5. Crucially, a reliable and durable delivery partner with likely longevity.

By opting for the ERC20 protocol and the Ethereum blockchain, Scotcoin have been able to achieve all five principles

85

APPENDIX 2

Different forms of validation for Blockchains

Proof of Work

A Proof-of-Work (PoW) system (or protocol, or function) is a measure to deter denial of service attacks and other service abuses such as spam on a network by requiring some work from the service requester, usually meaning processing time by a computer. The concept was invented by Cynthia Dwork and Moni Naor as presented in a 1993 journal article. The term "Proof of Work" or PoW was first coined and formalized in a 1999 paper by Markus Jakobsson and Ari Juels.

A key feature of these schemes is their asymmetry: the work must be moderately hard (but feasible) on the requester side but easy to check for the service provider.

Proof of Stake

Proof of stake (PoS) is a type of consensus algorithm by which a cryptocurrency blockchain network aims to achieve distributed consensus. In PoS-based crypto-currencies the creator of the next block is chosen via various combinations of random selection and wealth or age (i.e.,the stake). In contrast, the algorithm of proof-of-work-based cryptocurrencies such as bitcoin uses mining; that is, the solving of computationally intensive puzzles to validate transactions and create new blocks.

Kafka

Kafka is, in essence, a message handling system that uses the popular Publish-Subscribe model. Consumers subscribe to a Topic to receive new messages, that are published by the Producer. These topics, when they get bigger, are split into partitions, and Kafka guarantees that all messages inside a partition are sequentially ordered.

PoET

Sawtooth, like Fabric, is a permissioned blockchain network technology. The network is called permissioned because prospective participants must identify themselves to the network, and the network can decide whether to let them participate. Once in the network, participants share a view of the blockchain ledger. The network uses a consensus algorithm to make sure all participants see identical ledgers.

Consensus algorithms come in different forms. For example, Bitcoin uses a proof-of-work system. Members of the Bitcoin network compete to solve a cryptographic puzzle that identifies the solver as the new leader — the authoritative party for the new block on the blockchain. It's essentially a lottery for choosing who is responsible for adding the new block. Proof-of-stake is another lottery system, except the lottery is based on ownership of coin in the system. The more coin a participant owns, the more likely they are to be chosen as the leader for a new block.

In addition to lottery-like systems, there are also other kinds of consensus algorithms. For example, permissioned blockchain networks like Sawtooth and Fabric can also use traditional Byzantine fault tolerance (BFT) algorithms, which are often based on voting.

Sawtooth and Fabric are both designed to allow users to choose the consensus algorithm for their blockchain network. But there can be many variations; for example there is a lottery-like algorithm used with Hyperledger Sawtooth called proof-of-elapsed-time. (PoET)

APPENDIX 3

How to set up a Scotcoin Ethereum Wallet

You will need an Ethereum wallet to receive your new ScotcoinV3 tokens. If you already have a hardware Ethereum wallet please provide details of your wallet address for credit when buying Scotcoin. Your tokens will be credited to this address.

If you do not have an Ethereum wallet you will have to open one and provide us with your wallet address. The following information may be helpful but if you are unsure on how to open a wallet you should seek professional advice.

How to open an Ethereum wallet

There are various ways to create an Ethereum wallet and the most straightforward is Metamask. Metamask integrates directly with your browser and they have a very good two minute video showing the entire process titled: Getting Started with MetaMask, which you can serach for and find on YouTube.

Metamask is currently not available on Apple devices as it is on a limited trial. Once that trial is over it is possible Metamask will work very well on Apple devices. It works well with Firefox, Chrome and Brave.

There are also similar videos on the Scotcoin YouTube channel, and embedded at the Scotcoin website.

MyEtherWallet is one of the first Ethereum wallet

projects and is another trusted solution. Refer to their knowledge base at myetherwallet.com and decide if you want to use their website, phone app or extension.

Whatever solution you choose, your wallet must be ERC20 compatible (as the two recommended wallets above are).

For the avoidance of doubt, please be aware that it is your responsibility to ensure you provide Scotcoin with your correct wallet address as tokens sent to a wrong address provided by you cannot be resent.

APPENDIX 4

Famous Quotes on Digital Economy

"Bitcoin is a ponzi scheme" - Banks

"Internet will never scale" - Newspapers

"Uber isn't sustainable" - Taxis

"Airbnb won't work" - Hotels

"The swarm is headed towards us" – Satoshi Nakamoto, when WikiLeaks started accepting Bitcoin donation

"Bitcoin will do to banks what email did to the postal industry"– Rick Falkvinge, Founder of the Swedish pirate party

"I think the internet is going to be one of the major forces for reducing the role of government. The one thing that's missing but that will soon be developed, is a reliable e-cash." – Professor Milton Friedman, a Nobel Prize winner in economics

"Bitcoin seems to be a very promising idea. I like the idea of basing security on the assumption that the CPU power of honest participants outweighs that of the attacker. It is a very modern notion that exploits the power of the long tail." – Hal Finney

"It's money 2.0, a huge huge huge deal." – Chamath Palihapitiya, venture capitalist and early adopter of Bitcoin

"Bitcoin enables certain uses that are very unique. I think it offers possibilities that no other currency allows. For example the ability to spend a coin that only occurs when two separate parties agree to spend the coin; with a third party that couldn't run away with the coin itself." – Pieter Wuille

"Well, I think it is working. There may be other currencies like it that may be even better. But in the meantime, there's a big industry around Bitcoin. People have made fortunes off Bitcoin, some have lost money. It is volatile, but people make money off of volatility too."– Richard Branson

"Hey, obviously this is a very interesting time to be in Bitcoin right now, but if you guys want to argue over whether this is reality or not, one Bitcoin will feed over 40 homeless people in Pensacola right now. If you guys want proof Bitcoin is real, send them to me, I'll cash them out and feed homeless people." – Jason King

"Virtual Currencies may hold long-term promise, particularly if the innovations promote a faster, more secure and more efficient payment system."– Ben Bernanke (14th Chairman of the Federal Reserve, the Central Bank System of the United States)

"There are three eras of currency: Commodity based, politically based, and now, math based." – Chris Dixon

"There will be at most 21 million Bitcoins in existence. There isn't even enough BTC to go around for EVERY millionaire to own one. So before you buy any other coin (Litecoin included), try to own at least 1 BTC first." – Charlie Lee (Founder of Litecoin)

"I think the fact that within the Bitcoin universe an algorithm replaces the functions of the government is actually pretty cool. I am a big fan of Bitcoin." – Al Gore

"Blockchain is the tech. Bitcoin is merely the first mainstream manifestation of its potential." – Marc Kenigsberg

"You can't value Bitcoin because it's not a value-producing asset. [Bitcoin] itself is creating nothing. When you're buying non-productive assets, all you're counting on is the next person is going to pay you more because they're even more excited about another next person coming along. I can say almost with certainty that cryptocurrencies will come to a bad end," – Warren Buffett

"The currency isn't going to work. You can't have a business where people can invent a currency out of thin air and think that people who are buying it are really smart." – Jamie Dimon (JP Morgan Chase & Co)

"Bitcoin was created to serve a highly political intent, a free and uncensored network where all can participate with equal access." – Amir Taaki

"When I first heard about Bitcoin, I thought it was impossible. How can you have a purely digital currency? Can't I just copy your hard drive and have your bitcoins? I didn't understand how that could be done, and then I looked into it and it was brilliant" – Jeff Garzik

"As the value goes up, heads start to swivel and skeptics begin to soften. Starting a new currency is easy, anyone can do it. The trick is getting people to accept it, because it is their use that gives the "money" value." – Adam B. Levine

"At its core, bitcoin is a smart currency, designed by very forward-thinking engineers. It eliminates the need for banks, gets rid of credit card fees, currency exchange fees, money transfer fees, and reduces the need for lawyers in transitions… all good things" – Peter Diamandis

"Bitcoin is the currency of resistance." – Max Keiser

"Bitcoin, and the ideas behind it, will be a disrupter to the traditional notions of currency. In the end, currency will be better for it." – Edmund C. Moy

"There is so much potential, … I am just waiting for it to be a billion dollar industry." "Wow, Silk Road actually works" – Charlie Shrem

"Cryptocurrency Protocols Are Like Onions… One common design philosophy among many cryptocurrency 2.0 protocols is the idea that, just like the internet, cryptocurrency design would work best if protocols split off into different layers. Under this strain of thought, Bitcoin is to be thought of as a sort of TCP/IP of the cryptocurrency ecosystem, and other next-generation protocols can be built on top of Bitcoin much like we have SMTP for email, HTTP for webpages and XMPP for chat all on top of TCP as a common underlying data layer." – Vitalik Buterin

"The bitcoin world is this new ecosystem where it doesn't cost that much to start a new bitcoin company, it doesn't cost much to start owning bitcoin either, and it is a much more efficient way of moving money around the world." – Tim Draper

"I love seeing new services constantly starting to accept Bitcoin. Bitcoin is really becoming "the currency of the Internet." I'm most concerned by possible government reactions to Bitcoin. They can't destroy Bitcoin, but they could really slow things down by making exchange much more difficult." – Michael Marquardt

"Cryptocurrency is such a powerful concept that it can almost overturn governments" – Charlie Lee

"Spend some time with Bitcoin. Learn it, challenge it, and use it. You can assume no government wants you adopting this system in any capacity, and for that reason alone it's worth consideration by honest, moral, and industrious people" "Economists and journalists often get caught up in this question: Why does Bitcoin have value? And the answer is very easy. Because it is useful and scarce." – Erik Voorhees

"Will people be buying yachts with their Dogecoin riches some day? Probably not. But are we having a lot of fun, helping great causes and spreading the digital currency word in the process? Yes we are. And perhaps if we pool our Dogecoin together we can build a Dogeyacht and sail the world, just saying...!" – Jackson Palmer

"Bitcoin will do to banks what email did to the postal industry" – Rick Falkvinge, Founder of the Swedish pirate party

"I think the fact that within the bitcoin universe an algorithm replaces the functions of [the government] ... is actually pretty cool. I am a big fan of Bitcoin" – Al Gore, 45th Vice President of the United States

"I do think Bitcoin is the first [encrypted money] that has the potential to do something like change the world." – Peter Thiel, Co-Founder of Paypal

"So bitcoin is cyber snob currency..." – William Shatner, Actor known for lead role in Star Trek

"Bitcoin is a remarkable cryptographic achievement and the ability to create something that is not duplicable in the digital world has enormous value" – Eric Schmidt, CEO of Google

"Bitcoin is the most important invention in the history of the world since the Internet." – Roger Ver

"Money is a collective agreement. If enough people come to the same agreement, what they agree upon becomes secondary, whether it be farm animals, gold, diamonds, paper, or simply a code. History proves all these cases to be true. Who knows what the future is going to suggest to us as money, once we see digital currencies as ordinary?" – S.E. Sever, Writer

I understand the political ramifications of [Bitcoin] and I think that government should stay out of them and they should be perfectly legal." – Ron Paul, Republican Texas Congressman and former candidate for US President

"Cryptology represents the future of privacy [and] by implication [it] also represents the future of money, and the future of banking and finance." – Orlin Grabbe, Economist

"Gold is a great way to preserve wealth, but it is hard to move around. You do need some kind of alternative and Bitcoin fits the bill. I'm not surprised to see that happening." – Jim Rickards, American Lawyer, Economist and Investment Banker

"It's gold for nerds." – Stephen Colbert, American writer, comedian, television host, actor

"What can't kill Bitcoin, makes it (us) stronger." –

Mark Wittkowski, Online marketer, coach and pioneer in online lead generation.

"Bitcoin is a technological tour de force." – Bill Gates, Microsoft co-founder

"Every informed person needs to know about Bitcoin because it might be one of the world's most important developments." – Leon Luow, Nobel Peace prize nominee

"The relative success of the bitcoin proves that money first and foremost depends on trust. Neither gold nor bonds are needed to back up a currency." – Arnon Grunberg, Writer

"The governments of the world have spent hundreds and hundreds of trillions of dollars bailing out a decaying, dickensian, outmoded system called banking, when the solution to the future of finance is peer-to-peer. It's going to be alternative currencies like bitcoin and it's not actually going to be a banking system as we had before 2008." – Patrick Young, Financial analyst

"Instant transactions, no waiting for checks to clear, no chargebacks (merchants will like this), no account freezes (look out Paypal), no international wire transfer fee, no fees of any kind, no minimum balance, no maximum balance, worldwide access, always open, no waiting for business hours to make transactions, no waiting for an account to be approved before transacting, open an account in a few seconds, as easy as email, no bank account needed, extremely poor people can use it, extremely wealthy people can use it, no printing press, no hyper-inflation, no debt limit votes, no bank bailouts, completely voluntary. This sounds like the best payment system in the world!" – Trace Mayer J.D., a Leading Monetary Expert on Bitcoin and Gold

"You can't stop things like Bitcoin. It will be everywhere and the world will have to readjust. World governments will have to readjust" – John McAfee, Founder of McAfee

APPENDIX 5

The Howey Test

Why it is important is that ALL investment in the USA is judged against this test. Other countries (notably Canada and the UK in a rather tenuous way) are beginning to take the same line.

Reviewed by Jake Frankenfield
Updated Jun 25, 2019

Definition of Howey Test

The Securities Act of 1933 and the Securities Exchange Act of 1934 dictate much of the U.S. government's approach to financial regulation, even nearly 100 years after they were established. Under these acts, transactions which qualify as 'investment contracts' are considered securities, meaning that they are also subject to specific requirements related to disclosure and registration.

Predictably, this has a significant impact on how the financial world views and interacts with those securities, so it is necessary to have a consistent and thorough way of determining whether a transaction is, in fact, an example of an 'investment contract.'

The Howey Test is the standard methodology, put in place by the U.S. Supreme Court, to make that determination.

Breaking down theHowey Test

Put simply, the Howey Test asks whether the value of a transaction for one of its participants is dependent upon the other's work. Specifically, the Howey Test determines that a transaction represents an investment contract if "a person invests his money in a common enterprise and is led to expect profits solely from the efforts of the promoter or a third party,"

The Howey Test refers to a 1946 case which reached the Supreme Court, SEC v. W.J. Howey Co., a lawsuit involving the Howey Company of Florida. This company was a citrus farm which operated on a large swath of land in the southern portion of the state.

When the company decided to lease out half of its large property in order to "finance an additional development," the question of whether or not the land itself could be seen as a security came into play. Purchasers of the Howey land, who themselves had none of the "knowledge, skill, and equipment necessary for the care and cultivation of citrus trees," were speculators. They purchased the land based on the assumption that it would generate a profit for them as a result of the efforts of someone else.

Howey Co. ran afoul of the law when it failed to register the transactions. The U.S. Securities and Exchange Commission (SEC) responded with an injunction to block the sale of the land, and the case was eventually appealed, finally arriving in the U.S Supreme Court.

The opinion of the Court in the Howey case indicated that "the transactions in this case clearly involve investment contracts, as so defined. The respondent companies are offering something more than fee simple interests in land...they are offering an opportunity to contribute money and to share in the profits of a large citrus fruit enterprise."

In the case of Howey Co., the investors in the Florida land saw the transaction as valuable only because of the work that others would perform on the land. By the standards of the Howey Test, this classified the transaction as an investment contract. Thus, the transaction needed to be registered, and the Howey Co. was found to have violated the law by failing to do that.

Howey test being applied to crypto market

The Howey Test has remained a notable determiner of regulatory oversight for many decades. In the past few years, it has been called into question, most frequently in conjunction with discussions about cryptocurrencies and blockchain technology.

As investor activity in the cryptocurrency space has grown, the SEC has become increasingly interested in defining cryptocurrencies.

Digital currencies like Bitcoin are notoriously difficult to categorise in this way; they are decentralised and designed to evade regulation in many ways. Nonetheless, investors who have moved quickly to buy up the latest digital currency in the hopes of turning a profit are undoubtedly engaging in behavior that could be characterised as speculation.

From the perspective of the Howey Test, the

operative question in this case is whether or not cryptocurrency investors are participating in a speculative enterprise, and if so, if the profits those investors are hoping for are entirely dependent upon the work of a third party.

If the SEC determines that a particular cryptocurrency token is classified as a security, that brings about a host of implications for that cryptocurrency. Effectively, it means the SEC can determine whether or not the token can be sold to U.S. investors legally or not; it also compels U.S. investors to register their token holdings with the SEC.

There are parallels between the cryptocurrency world and the original Howey Co. situation, but there are also many differences. Critically, cryptocurrencies are autonomous and distributed networks that are designed to be decentralised. Classifying a cryptocurrency as a security likely goes sharply against the goals of the creators of that digital currency.

However, considering how significant the cryptocurrency space has become, the SEC has a growing interest in monitoring and overseeing cryptocurrency transactions in a way that it sees as appropriate. Regardless of the ultimate regulatory decision, it is sure to have a significant impact on the virtual currency world and investors in that space.

APPENDIX 6

Bitcoin block sizes, problems and history

What are blocks?

A block comprises a file in which data pertaining to the most recent transactions on the Bitcoin network is permanently recorded. Each block can be likened to a page of a ledger, with the blocks "chaining" together to comprise the decentralised ledger that underpins the Bitcoin network.

Those bundled transactions are confirmed by miners before they are added to the Bitcoin blockchain as new blocks. The size of a block creates a limit on the number of transactions that can be verified with each block. As such, larger blocks require greater computation power and will take longer to be mined. Blocks exceeding the limit will be rejected by the network.

During Bitcoin's infancy, blocks were limited to carry no more than 36 megabytes of transaction data each. However, the block size was reduced to 1 MB on July 14, 2010 in order to counter both the threat of transactional spam clogging up the network and potential distributed denial-of-service (DDoS) attacks.

However, universal consensus regarding an ideal block size was not found, and core developers predicted that the rate of transactions hosted by the network may exceed the available block space in future, arguing in favour of an increase to the 1 MB limit shortly after it was put in place. Since the introduction of the 1 MB block limit, the number of transactions processed per second by the BTC network has largely oscillated between two and seven.

Why does block size matter?

The size of a block imposes a limit on the number of transactions that the Bitcoin network is capable of processing per second and thus can be seen to inhibit the network's ability to scale. When blocks fill, the network becomes congested, and transaction fees rise dramatically.

At the start of 2013, the average Bitcoin block size was approximately 125 kilobytes. By May 2015, increasing adoption had led to a 240% rise in block size since 2013 — from 125 KB to roughly 425 KB — however, crypto trade tool provider TradeBlock then estimated that blocks were hitting the 1 MB limit at least four times daily on average.

By 2015, the increasing prevalence of blocks near the limit of transactional data began to pervade the mainstream cryptocurrency zeitgeist, with concerns pertaining to a significant slowdown in the processing of transactions and an increase in fees being brought to the fore.

The resulting increased fees and delays in the processing of transactions were seen to undermine the core utilities underpinning BTC, with many within the community concerned that network congestion and an increase in the cost of transfers would render Bitcoin redundant as a means of exchange.

At the time, TradeBlock estimated that "at least some otherwise-acceptable transactions are seeing delayed confirmations due to capacity issues on the network 3% of the time since the beginning of the year."

Why increase the block size?

Over the years, Bitcoin has seen numerous proposals advocating that an increase is needed in order to reduce fees, process more transactions per second, and allow Bitcoin to scale to compete with mainstream payments technologies.

On May 4, 2015, Gavin Andresen published an article titled "Why increasing the max block size is urgent," further escalating the perceived gravity of the block size debate, despite the average BTC block then being only 30-40% full. Andresen warned:

> "If the number of transactions waiting gets large enough, the end result will be an over-saturated network, busy doing nothing productive. I don't think that is likely — it is more likely people just stop using Bitcoin because transaction confirmation becomes increasingly unreliable."

Later that month, Andresen asserted that he would shift his work toward alternative client Bitcoin XT should the community fail to reach consensus regarding the implementation of a block size increase. The 0.10 version of Bitcoin XT had been launched during December 2014 by Bitcoin Core developer and prominent critic of the 1 MB block limit Mike Hearn.

On June 4, 2015, Andresen advocated that the miners

and node operators should be able to autonomously decide the size of blocks, arguing that the community should either maintain the limit and "see how high transactions fees must rise until miners realise they're 'leaving money on the table' and raise the block max size themselves" or alternatively "replace the limit with a 'go along with the crowd' rule that means any miner that doesn't care will create blocks that neither increase nor decrease the average block size."

On June 12, 2015, a statement requesting the introduction of 8 MB blocks that had been signed by major Chinese mining pools F2pool, BTCChina, Antpool, Huobi and BW surfaced online, indicating transnational demand for larger blocks.

On June 22, 2015, Andresen published Bitcoin Improvement Proposal (BIP) 101, which advocated "replacing the fixed one-megabyte maximum block size with a maximum size that grows over time at a predictable rate."

What was BIP101?

BIP101 proposed that the maximum block size be raised to 8 MB as of Jan. 11, 2016, before increasing linearly to double every 730 days until January 2036.

The 8 MB limit was estimated to be able to facilitate the processing of 24 transactions per second. The BIP101 proposal was well-received by large segments of the public, including leading Chinese mining pools.

However, the Bitcoin community remained divided on the issue of block size, with Bram Cohen, the creator of

Bittorrent, publishing an article titled "Bitcoin's Ironic Crisis" on June 23, 2015, in which Cohen argued in favor of transactions fees being determined by market forces amid the maintenance of the 1 MB block limit:

> "The proposed 'solution' to the 'problem' of hitting the transaction rate limit is to raise the limit from 1 megabyte to 20 megabytes. This sort of change flies directly in the face of the ethos of Bitcoin."

Cohen asserted that the prevalence of high fees would evidence Bitcoin to be "providing real value" and emphasized the incentive such an option would offer to miners in exchange for securing the network. Furthermore, Cohen added:

> "In the long term the mining rewards for Bitcoin will go away completely (there's a strict schedule for this) and all that's left will be transaction fees. Attempting to 'solve' the problem of transaction fees would in the long run undermine the security of Bitcoin even if it were done perfectly."

On Aug. 16, 2015, Andresen's BIP101 was merged into the code of Bitcoin XT. Despite BIP101 receiving widespread support from the crypto community, the inclusion of BIP101 into Bitcoin XT's protocol failed to spark widespread adoption of the alternative client. During the second half of 2015, users of Bitcoin XT alleged that they were the victims of a coordinated attack against the chain. So, which block size increase proposals garnered community support?

Bitcoin XT, Bitcoin Unlimited, Bitcoin Classic and Segwit2x were among the initiatives to increase Bitcoin block size that received the greatest community support during 2016, but none have succeeded in forcing a block size increase.

In January 2016, BIP101 was removed from Bitcoin XT's protocol in favor of a one-time block size increase to 2 MB, which preceded the rapid collapse of support for Bitcoin XT. By January 2017, less than 30 Bitcoin XT nodes were maintained by miners — down from approximately 650 one year prior. Despite the collapse of Bitcoin XT, proposals in favor of a block size increase proliferated, such as Bitcoin Unlimited, which was launched in January 2015 and allowed users to signal block sizes.

At the time, Bitcoin Classic emerged as the means to a block size increase that appeared to garner the greatest community support following its launch on Feb. 10, 2016. The proposed fork would support a one-time 2 MB block size increase, with the Wall Street Journal's Paul Vigna describing the proposal as having "emerged from the ashes of the XT/Core debate." Despite appearing to quickly gain support, Bitcoin Classic failed to attract support from more than 75% of miners and, as such, failed to emerge as the dominant chain. Bitcoin Classic would eventually cease operations after the project's developers pledged support for the Bitcoin Cash chain during 2017.

APPENDIX 7

What is 'halving' in Bitcoin and other cryptos?

In Bitcoin, halving is when block rewards for mining are cut in half. Halving happens at regular intervals based on the Bitcoin protocol.

Many other cryptos mined in the style of Bitcoin (proof-of-work mining) are subject to halving as well. With that in mind, coins have unique mechanisms for slowing down block rewards.

In other words, in terms of coins that work like Bitcoin, for example Litecoin, the code underlying the network dictates that X new coins minted as mining rewards for miners adding blocks of transactions to the blockchain will be cut in half every Y blocks until the reward reaches zero and no new coins are mined.

With Bitcoin, halving occurs every 210,000 blocks. Since one block is added to the Bitcoin blockchain roughly every 10 minutes, each halving is about 210,000 block, or four years apart.

When is the next Bitcoin halving? Bitcoin started by giving 50 Bitcoin per block produced. That went to 25, then 12.5 and currently sits at 6.25 BTC per completed block. Halving takes place roughly ever four years so the next halving, which will reduce the reward 3.125 BTC per completed block, will be in May 2024

Will Bitcoin's price be affected by the halving?

The correlation between halvings and price has been positive so far in Bitcoin's history... but of course, the past doesn't tell us anything about the future with certainty.

APPENDIX 8

Blockchain Q&A

What does a decentralised Blockchain mean?

A blockchain is exactly what it says it is – a chain of linked blocks of data. Being decentralised means that all the information in any given block is immediately transmitted to all the nodes (computers) in the system. More than 51% of these nodes have to confirm a transaction for it to be marked as correct. So there are lots of people who confirm, ie it is not one party confirmation

What is a smart contract?

Long answer! And I'm indebted to Margaret Rouse for it. A smart contract, also known as a cryptocontract, is a computer program that directly controls the transfer of digital currencies or assets between parties under certain conditions. A smart contract not only defines the rules and penalties related to an agreement in the same way that a traditional contract does, but it can also automatically enforce those obligations.

It does this by taking in information as input, assigning a value to that input through the rules set out in the contract and executing the actions required by those contractual clauses -- for example, determining whether an asset should go to one person or should be returned to the other person from whom the asset originated.

These contracts are stored on blockchain technology,

a decentralised ledger that also underpins Bitcoin and other cryptocurrencies.

What smart contracts do

Smart contracts are complex, and their potential goes beyond the simple transfer of assets -- they can execute transactions in a wide range of fields, from legal processes to insurance premiums to crowdfunding agreements to financial derivatives. Smart contracts have the potential to disintermediate the legal and financial fields; in particular, by simplifying and automating routine and repetitive processes for which people currently pay lawyers and banks sizable fees.

The role of lawyers could also shift in the future as smart contracts gain traction in areas from adjudicating traditional legal contracts to producing customizable smart contract templates. Additionally, smart contracts' ability not only to automate processes, but also to control behaviour, as well as their potential with real-time auditing and risk assessments, can be beneficial to compliance.

Smart contract history and creation

The notion of smart contracts was first proposed by Nick Szabo in 1994. Szabo is a legal scholar and cryptographer known for laying the groundwork for digital currency. Back then, there was little interest or activity in smart contracts because there was no digital platform or distributed ledger that could support them.

In 2009, the cryptocurrency Bitcoin was developed via

a blockchain platform comprised of a digital and distributed ledger that tracks monetary transactions. This technology enabled the development of smart contract code that is used to enter all the terms of the contract into the blockchain.

Many platforms now allow for the use of smart contracts, including Ethereum, bitcoin and Nxt. Today, with the growing adoption of bitcoin and the support of blockchain technologies, smart contracts are growing in popularity, often built on top of digital currencies to trigger payments.

Smart contract applications and blockchain

Blockchain is ideal for storing smart contracts because of the technology's security and immutability. Smart contract data is encrypted on a shared ledger, making it impossible to lose the information stored in the blocks.

Another advantage of blockchain technology being incorporated into smart contracts is flexibility. Developers are able to store almost any type of data within a blockchain, and they have a wide variety of transaction options to choose from during smart contract deployment. In many ways a smart contract could be described as a form of "Super Escrow"

Is it possible to hack a Blockchain?

No. The cryptographic nature of the blockchain (any blockchain) means it is unhackable. That is not to say that the exchange through which transactions are channelled cannot be hacked. Indeed they regularly are. This is because the exchanges are not themselves part of a blockchain, but essentially a single point of failure that can be attacked

What different types of blockchains are there?

All blockchains have the same basic characteristics ie they are blocks of data linked in a chain. There are differences in the way they operate, but they all essentially do the same thing – store large amounts of data in a way that cannot be changed or dropped.

What is double spending?

The potential flaw that can occur in a digital cash scheme which results in spending the same digital token twice. A digital token differs from physical cash because it consists of a digital file that can be duplicated of falsified. When dealing with counterfeit money, such occurrences create new amounts of copied currency which did not previously exist. Inflation devalues the currency and diminishes user trust as well as circulation and retention of the currency. Blind signatures are fundamental cryptographic techniques that prevent double-spending while upholding transaction anonymity.

Will central banks use blockchains to create their own cryptocurrency?

The likelihood is that they will. At the moment there is a

great stirring and mixing of regulation (both for and against) within all jurisdictions, but essentially the blockchain offers so many advantages that in time it is unlikely that any central authority will be able to stand apart. There is already a bank to bank crypto currency called Ripple (XRP) which is having some success in driving interbank transactions. But not all banks are engaged and not all banks want to be engaged

When will blockchains become mainstream?

Arguably they are already there. Many industries are moving from what (for lack of a better expression) is effectively Excel sheet data handling to Blockchain data handling. Blockchain is by far and away the best way to store and collate data. There are huge numbers of legacy systems, but in time I suspect they will all change over to some form of blockchain data handling

In what way are Blockchains transparent?

Anyone can go to programs called block explorers and see exactly what transactions have occurred. You can't see the name and address of people who are transacting, but you can see the wallet addresses.

The best known block explorer is found at blockchain.com/explorer, which shows every single transaction as it happens on the Bitcoin blockchain, as well as details of all the blocks, with the latest ones being shown as they are completed. You will also find there, the transaction hash fore every single transaction.

The transaction hash is the unique reference for every single transaction and this is logged, also. The block number is the block in the chain that holds this transaction. A new block is created approximately every ten minutes. Time, asset and quantity are also shown. The coin is shown as transferring from one wallet to another (destination). And finally on the block explorer, you will see the status, of every transaction, usually 'valid', although this might be pending or rejected also.

Is DLT and Blockchain the same thing?

Yes and no. A blockchain is created by the use of DLT (distributed leger technology). DLT means that the information is broadcast to all the nodes on the system. A node is really just a computer, and there are tens of thousands in the Bitcoin blockchain for example. The spreading of all the data around the system means it is distributed. The blockchain stores the ledger that is created in this way

Can blocks be removed from a Blockchain?

That's a simple one! No. Once the chain is formed, the block created (in fact any block) cannot be removed from the chain

How does consensus algorithms work?

The algorithms that are used in the blockchain are extremely complex cryptographic mathematical calculations. They become steadily more complex as time goes on. The nodes (computers) work to solve the equations that are created. When a solution is found, that means the block is complete and the data is immutably fixed

How is Blockchain data stored?

In the same way that computers store data using a language, the Blockchain does the same thing. The difference is it can't be changed. Any data can be copied, changed, erased or expanded unless it is on a blockchain. If it is, once the block has been created and confirmed the data is stored forever and immutable, and precisely date and time stamped

What professions will be affected the most by the growth of Blockchain technology?

Blockchain is best at handling large amounts of data, storing it, timestamping it and making it impossible to change. Although several industries will be utterly changed, it doesn't necessarily mean they will employ any less people. For example, in the legal world, smart contracts will take much of the drudgery out of property transactions. But there will still have to be people actually writing the specific contracts, which is not so different from what happens now.

Similarly, accountants, whose main job is making sure lots of invoices and payments are real, won't need to do that. The blockchain confirms they are real and correct.

But the putting together of final accounts will still require specialised input, and the interpretation of those accounts will still need to be done by qualified experts. But perhaps the greatest changes will be with the banks, where online and cashless is already taking its toll. Blockchain has the capacity to reduce their costs dramatically, but at the same time to reduce what they can charge, possibly by even more. The legacy of the past will fight to the last, but Capitalism will always drive out the inefficient in the end.

APPENDIX 9

Tax and Regulation of Crypto Assets in the UK

On December 15, 2017, the European Council and the European Parliament finally agreed the 5th AML (Anti Money Laundering) Directive. This directive contains the first legally binding definition of virtual currencies and is the most significant regulatory action over virtual currencies anywhere in the world. Because of a Swedish ruling a couple of years ago, recently upheld by the ECJ (European Court of Justice), virtual currency transactions are exempt from VAT according to the current EU laws and regulations. The binding force of case law of the ECJ is recognised without objection by all EU member states & courts i.e. virtual currencies are exempt from VAT across all jurisdictions of EU member states. At present UK does not recognise cryptos as either currency or commodity. It is certain the UK authorities will make a determination at some point in the future.

The UK leads in Fintech innovation, as the place to be for financial entrepreneurs; however, cryptocurrency regulation in the UK is behind others. All issuance of equity and debt are regulated by the FCA (Financial Conduct Authority) whose aim is seamless operation of financial markets, by providing protection for consumers and investors, plus promoting effective competition in markets. The FCA maintains that "cryptoassets designed primarily as a means of payment or exchange do not sit within the scope of FCA authority." While SEC and

CFTC engage in crypto market regulation in the U.S, virtual currencies are mostly unregulated in the UK. The FCA doesn't consider virtual currencies to be currencies or commodities under the MiFID II (markets in financial instruments directive) and, therefore, has no jurisdiction over them. It has authority over activities related to virtual currency derivatives such as bitcoin futures, options, or crypto-linked ETFs (if approved). The FCA's position is ambivalent. On the one hand, the FCA never explicitly declared authority over security offerings in the form of ICOs/STOs, but on the other, it issues consumer warnings describing ICOs as "very-high-risk speculative investments" and unhelpful statements such as "Whether an ICO falls within the FCA's regulatory boundaries or not can only be decided case by case." Difficult to navigate that one…However, come January 2021, all businesses involved with Crypto currency in any form will have to be registered with the FCA.

Regulatory Authorities in the UK intend to apply AML (Anti Money Laundering) regulations in order to comply with the EU's 5th AML Directive. Along the same lines, the Treasury has revealed their intentions to regulate cryptocurrency traders, requiring them to abide by KYC (Know Your Customer) regulations and disclose their identities as well as report suspicious activities. On tax though the UK is ahead of the game. In 2014, HMRC published guidance regarding the tax treatment of virtual currencies. The UK was one of, if not the first country, to have a clear legal position on the issue – albeit "for tax purposes only." HMRC guidelines clarify that: (i) mining income is not subject to VAT, (ii) any loss or gain arising from the holding and/or selling of virtual currencies will be treated in the same way as gains made in other commodities or currencies, (iii) virtual currencies acquired and held for personal reasons instead of speculative purposes will probably not be subject to capital gains tax. You can compare this with buying a painting and sticking it on your wall rather than popping it into Sothebys. The UK authorities are under pressure to produce a comprehensive strategy on virtual currencies as soon as possible. Other EU countries are currently ahead in legislative support. Theresa May, whilst Prime Minister, has suggested the UK might follow South Korea in banning anonymous trading and regulating exchanges. On a related note, the World Bank sees the further enhanced development of blockchain as fundamental to cryptocurrency development, and also pure blockchain development

APPENDIX 10

Useful information

Security tools:

Your password is the first line of defence for your security and please stop using the same password everywhere. You are responsible for the security of your wallet and passwords. Since you are into cryptocurrency world, you need to be smart and ahead of hackers. Here are the things that will help.

Browser:

● Brave browser: This is the most preferred browser for crypto users. It is privacy centric and stop websites from tracking you. You can also install Chrome add-ons in this browser. It is however faster than Chrome and available for desktop and mobile as well.

● Tor Browser: This browser is better than a VPN but is a little slow in speed. It is however a reliable browser for hiding your IP.

Password management tool:

● Dashlane: This helps you generate a new password and saves it automatically. When you log in to the site the next time, it automatically fills the username and password. Not only does it save a lot of time, but it also increases your security. The mobile app is pretty solid too. Make a habit and start using it from today.

• MetaCert Chrome add-on: This tool saves you from phishing pages. Absolutely must have!

Wallet:

• Ledger Nano X: The best way to keep your Bitcoin and 100+ other cryptocurrencies safe. These physical wallets which plug into your device via USB also support ERC 20 coin and Binance chain coins.

• TrustWallet: If you are looking for a mobile wallet, use Edge. However, nothing beats the security offered by a hardware wallet.

• Exodus wallet: Desktop wallet. Use this as a last resort only. Do remember, your desktop and mobile can easily be hacked whereas hardware wallets ensure your coins remain safe.

Best Exchanges for Crypto:

• Coinbase: While the cryptocurrency industry has had issues with fraudulent coins and shady exchanges, Coinbase has avoided any controversy. Coinbase is extremely easy-to-use and lowers the barrier to entry for cryptocurrency investment. Coinbase also offers insured custodial wallets for investors and traders to store their investments. They carry insurance against data breaches and hacking and your cash is stored in FDIC insured bank accounts. These custodial accounts are convenient for newer users, but the private keys to the coins within them are owned by Coinbase, and not the investor. Coinbase does however make buying and selling cryptocurrencies easy with strong security and transparent pricing.

- Binance: The #1 Altcoin exchange with a great mobile app.

- Bit.it: Popular exchange.

- KuCoin: Another good exchange which is coming up with many new features.

- Changelly: Not an exchange but if you want to get any new coin instantly, this is a great website.

APPENDIX 11

Digital Asset Exchanges Explained

Human beings are a species of traders, it's second nature. Everyone has something the other wants, and trading is the solution to it. The same applies to the global digital currency markets. What drives the value of the digital currencies is the same as for any other commodity, supply and demand. The greater the demand the higher the value, the same way as an increase in supply results in devaluation. When trading on the digital currency markets one must understand bid and ask prices, as well as the two most important order types, market and limit orders.

Digital currencies are usually traded on an exchange where both the buyer and seller set the price. The bid price is the price the buyer is willing to pay and the ask price is what the seller is willing to sell at. There are other elements that count as well and to make money on what is still a volatile market one needs knowledge and experience. The most important rule is to never put in more money than you can afford to lose.

Digital currency exchanges are a crypto version of a stock exchange and there are currently over 200 exchanges globally. They all range in fees, services and legitimacy so it is important to find one with a proven track record before you begin trading. As an initiative to clean up the crypto space, BTI launched a cryptocurrency exchange verification service. Some exchanges have been exposed for wash trading – the process of buying digital currency with one broker while selling it with another, which results in misleading information. BTI uses a wash trade algorithm to determine wash traded volumes and awards exchanges with less than 10% volumes with the BTI verification.

In order to analyze and play the market, you will need to understand trading techniques and terminology. This is where market and limit orders come into play.

Market Order

A market order is an order to buy or sell at the best available price and is usually executed immediately. It is considered to be the best way for new traders to get started because you can easily get in and out of a trade.

Limit Order

Unlike the market order, with this order type is that you can determine the price, which is also its biggest advantage. Though it is not guaranteed that it will be executed, as it depends on the market price. A buy limit order can therefore only be executed at the limit price or lower, and a sell limit order can only be executed at the limit price or higher.

The legislation around cryptocurrency exchanges differs between countries, but most exchanges follow regulations related to the protection of the customer. That is the anti-money laundering laws (AML) and know your customer laws (KYC). There are three types of cryptocurrency exchanges; centralized, decentralised and hybrids.

Centralised exchanges

The centralised exchange is the most common type of exchanges for cryptocurrencies and they are similar to traditional stock exchanges. It handles the transaction and matches the buyer and the seller, for a fee. There are two significant downsides of the centralized exchange, first of all their vulnerability to hackers and secondly the fact that the exchange holds your assets in a hosted wallet, which means that if the exchange goes under you lose your assets.

Decentralised Exchanges

The decentralized exchanges adapt the original philosophy of cryptocurrencies being traded through peer-to-peer transactions without a middle man involved. Decentralised exchanges are extremely difficult to hack and all transactions are conducted via smart contracts which keep trading fees low. On the downside it can be a vulnerability to have complete control of your own assets.

Hybrid Exchanges

If you merge the concept of the centralised exchange with the decentralised exchange you get a hybrid exchange, the potential to get the best of both exchange types. Just like the decentralised system, a hybrid creates smart contracts to ensure the integrity of the trade but the hybrid also provides the functionality of a centralized exchange and provides liquidity. There is a growing amount of hybrid exchanges on the market.

There is no one-size-fits-all type of exchange. It all comes down to the individual needs and requirements. Whichever exchange you decide to use, I would always recommend that the majority of your holdings be under your own secure custody.

Happy trading!

APPENDIX 12

What Is A Ponzi Scheme & Why Bitcoin Is Not One

by zSudhir Khatwani

One of the biggest myths regarding Bitcoin is that many consider it as a fraudulent Ponzi scheme. But very few actually understand what a Ponzi scheme is.

It is not wise for people to draw conclusions without a proper understanding of any topic whatsoever. And that is what people are doing when it comes to Bitcoins. They just term Bitcoins and other cryptos as scams.

Therefore, I think it is very important for us to clarify this point and spread more awareness, which is also my motivation to write today. I will explain in detail why Bitcoin is not a Ponzi scheme, but before that let's understood and examine what a Ponzi scheme actually means.

What Is A Ponzi Scheme?

A Ponzi scheme is a fraudulent investment operation where the operator generates returns for older investors through revenue paid by new investors, rather than from legitimate business activities or profit from financial trading.

Operators of Ponzi schemes can be either individuals or corporations and they grab the attention of new investors by offering short-term returns that are either abnormally high or otherwise unusually consistent.

Companies and people that engage in Ponzi schemes focus all of their energy into attracting new clients to make investments. Ponzi schemes rely on a constant flow of new investments to continue to provide returns to older investors. When this flow runs out, the scheme falls apart.

Ponzi schemes are sometimes also referred as pyramid schemes and the characteristics of both the schemes are higher returns than the average market by recruiting new members under the scheme and taking money from them in some form or other.

Characteristics of Ponzi or Pyramid Schemes:

- They promise high and unusual returns.
- They promise regular or monthly returns usually.
- They require you to add new investors /members into the scheme to increase your return rate.
- Founders usually run away with a big chunk of money.

These are the main characteristics of a typical fraudulent scheme whether it is in the crypto space or otherwise.

Now that you know these characteristics you can easily do away with such schemes by doing a quick litmus test. You can quickly do a litmus test to avoid such schemes or projects by following two simple bits of advice given by Andreas M. Antonopoulos, a renowned Bitcoin speaker, and proponent.

Andreas M. Antonopoulos (Dec 1, 2017):

Does it promise regular returns that exceed average market returns?
It's a Ponzi

Does it focus more on recruiting new people than any product?
It's a pyramid scheme

This litmus test is so powerful and apt that you can apply it within the crypto space. You can also use it to judge other schemes outside of this market.

Bitcoin Is Not A Ponzi Scheme

In the light of the above explanations, I can say that people who say Bitcoin is a Ponzi scheme don't really understand what a Ponzi scheme is.

Bitcoin never asked anyone to buy it

The Bitcoin whitepaper, if you have read it, doesn't say a thing about buying and selling Bitcoins and nor does it try to lure investors to put their money into anything. It is an eight page document explaining a solution for making a censorship-resistant digital money.

On top of that, the Bitcoin founder, Satoshi Nakamoto never ran away with a chunk of Bitcoins. One might now argue that he held millions of Bitcoins but that he never stole from anybody or just created out of thin air despite being Bitcoin's founder.

Instead, he also had to run a full node and mine Bitcoin blocks to receive the block rewards to get new bitcoins, which is a legal way that anyone can follow even today.

Also, note that the Bitcoins he mined at that time and kept to himself were worthless then. It was his sheer will to believe in the potential of the project that motivated him to keep those funds with him.

Also, Bitcoin never asked you to recruit new people or investors under it

Neither Satoshi nor his whitepaper or even early Bitcoin holders went to recruit new people or investors for Bitcoin.

In initial days, mostly geeks used to mine and play with Bitcoin and most of them used to spend it on gambling or pizzas, or they just used to givea it way in meetups. I have not seen such Ponzi scheme yet that give away their products in such a manner.

Next, Bitcoin doesn't promise or give any kind of regular returns.

The Bitcoin whitepaper or its working model to date doesn't promise any returns or regular returns either. Of course, people have made money due to the wild rises and falls in the price of Bitcoin over the years but that's simply the law of demand and supply acting in a free market.

On the flip side, the Bitcoin prices also falls rapidly and many people get burned due to their such speculative investment!.

Finally, Bitcoin has no head or person controlling it

Bitcoin is based on the decentralised and censorship-resistant tech of blockchain and proof of work which makes sure that no one, in particular, is 'in-charge'.

Clearly, with no one at the helm of Bitcoin, no one can run away or take over other people's money or Bitcoin.

Conclusion: Crypto-Scams

Everything said and done, I understand that there are a lot of cryptocurrency Ponzi schemes and pyramid schemes going on but that doesn't mean Bitcoin or the other currencies are fraudulent.

On the flip side, cryptocurrency market has been, is, and will be prone to such schemes because it is based on the decentralised technology of blockchain. Something which is based on decentralised tech and is hard to stop or regulate will give birth to Ponzi schemes but that doesn't mean that Bitcoin is a Ponzi scheme.

Instead, use the parameters that I have discussed at the start of this article to educate and examine yourself whenever you encounter such Ponzi schemes and simply opt out of it.

Lastly, I would say, I am yet to see a Ponzi scheme like Bitcoin which does this:

Show me a ponzi scheme where the early investors donated $86 Million to charity and I'll give you all my #bitcoins. (Miguel Cuneta)

APPENDIX 13

The Blockchain Economy: A beginner's guide to institutional cryptoeconomics

Chris Berg, Sinclair Davidson and Jason Potts are from the RMIT Blockchain Innovation Hub, the world's first social science research centre into the economics, politics, sociology, and law of blockchain technology.

The blockchain is a digital, decentralised, distributed ledger.

Most explanations for the importance of the blockchain start with Bitcoin and the history of money. But money is just the first use case of the blockchain. And it is unlikely to be the most important.

It might seem strange that a ledger — a dull and practical document associated mainly with accounting — would be described as a revolutionary technology. But the blockchain matters because ledgers matter.

Ledgers all the way down

Ledgers are everywhere. Ledgers do more than just record accounting transactions. A ledger consists simply of data structured by rules. Any time we need a consensus about facts, we use a ledger. Ledgers record the facts underpinning the modern economy.

Ledgers confirm ownership. Property title registers map who owns what and whether their land is subject to any caveats or encumbrances. Hernando de Soto has documented how the poor suffer when they own property that has not been confirmed in a ledger. The firm is a ledger, as a network of ownership, employment and production relationships with a single purpose. A club is a ledger, structuring who benefits and who does not.

Ledgers confirm identity. Businesses have identities recorded on government ledgers to track their existence and their status under tax law. The register of Births Deaths and Marriages records the existence of individuals at key moments, and uses that information to confirm identities when those individuals are interacting with the world.

Ledgers confirm status. Citizenship is a ledger, recording who has the rights and is subject to obligations due to national membership. The electoral roll is a ledger, allowing (and, in Australia, obliging) those who are on that roll a vote. Employment is a ledger, giving those employed a contractual claim on payment in return for work.

Ledgers confirm authority. Ledgers identify who can validly sit in parliament, who can access what bank account, who can work with children, who can enter restricted areas.

At their most fundamental level, ledgers map economic and social relationships.

Agreement about the facts and when they change — that is, a consensus about what is in the ledger, and a trust that the ledger is accurate — is one of the fundamental bases of market capitalism.

Ownership, possession, and ledgers

Let's make a distinction here that is crucial but easy to miss: between ownership and possession.

Take passports. Each country asserts the right to control who crosses its borders, and each country maintains a ledger of which of its citizens have the right to travel. A passport is a physical item — call it a token — that refers back to this ledger.

In the pre-digital world, possession indicated ownership of that right. The Australian passport ledger consisted of index cards held in by the government of each state. Border agents presented with a passport could surmise that the traveller who held it was listed on a distant ledger as allowed to travel. Of course this left border control highly exposed to fraud.

Possession implies ownership, but possession is not ownership. Now modern passports allow the authorities to confirm ownership directly. Their digital features allow airlines and immigration authorities to query the national passport database and determine that a passenger is free to travel.

Passports are a relatively straightforward example of this distinction. But as Bitcoin has shown: money is a ledger, too.

Possession of a banknote token indicates ownership. In the nineteenth century the possessor — 'bearer' — of a banknote had a right to draw on the issuing bank the value of the note. These banknotes were direct liabilities for the issuing bank, and were recorded on the banks' ledger. A regime of possession indicating ownership

143

meant that banknotes were susceptible to be both stolen and forged.

In our era fiat currencies a five dollar bill cannot be returned to the central bank for gold. But the relationship remains — the value of the bill is dependent on a social consensus about the stability of the currency and government that issued it. Banknotes are not wealth, as Zimbabweans and Yugoslavians and Weimar Republic Germans have unfortunately learned. A bill is a call on a relationship in a (now synthetic) ledger and if that relationship collapses, so does the value of the bill.

The evolution of the ledger

For all its importance, ledger technology has been mostly unchanged ... until now.

Ledgers appear at the dawn of written communication. Ledgers and writing developed simultaneously in the Ancient Near East to record production, trade, and debt. Clay tablets baked with cuneiform script detailed units of rations, taxes, workers and so forth. The first international 'community' was arranged through a structured network of alliances that functioned a lot like a distributed ledger.

The first major change to ledgers appeared in the fourteenth century with the invention of double entry bookkeeping. By recording both debits and credits, double entry bookkeeping conserved data across multiple (distributed) ledgers, and allowed for the reconciliation of information between ledgers.

The nineteenth century saw the next advance in ledger

technology with the rise of large corporate firms and large bureaucracies. These centralised ledgers enabled dramatic increases in organisational size and scope, but relied entirely on trust in the centralised institutions.

In the late twentieth century ledgers moved from analog to digital ledgers. For example, in the 1970s the Australian passport ledger was digitised and centralised. A database allows for more complex distribution, calculation, analysis and tracking. A database is computable and searchable.

But a database still relies on trust; a digitised ledger is only as reliable as the organisation that maintains it (and the individuals they employ). It is this problem that the blockchain solves. The blockchain is a distributed ledger that does not rely on a trusted central authority to maintain and validate the ledger.

Blockchain and the economic institutions of capitalism

The economic structure of modern capitalism has evolved in order to service these ledgers.

Oliver Williamson, the 2009 Nobel laureate in economics, argued that people produce and exchange in markets, firms, or governments depending on the relative transactions costs of each institution. Williamson's transactions cost approach provides a key to understanding what institutions manage ledgers and why.

Governments maintain ledgers of authority, privilege, responsibility and access. Governments are the trusted entity that keeps databases of citizenship and the right to travel, taxation obligations, social security entitlements, and property ownership. Where a ledger requires coercion in order to be enforced, the government is required.

Firms also maintain ledgers: proprietary ledgers of employment and responsibility, of the ownership and deployment of physical and human capital, of suppliers and customers, of intellectual property and corporate privilege. A firm is often described as a 'nexus of contracts'. But the value of the firm comes from the way that nexus is ordered and structured — the firm is in fact a ledger of contracts and capital.

Firms and governments can use blockchains to make their work more efficient and reliable. Multinational firms and networks of firms need to reconcile transactions on a global basis and blockchains can allow them to do so near-instantaneously. Governments can use the immutability of the blockchain to guarantee that property titles and identity records are accurate and untampered. Well-designed permissioning rules on blockchain applications can give citizens and consumers more control over their data.

But blockchains also compete against firms and governments. The blockchain is an institutional technology. It is a new way to maintain a ledger — that is, coordinate economic activity — distinct from firms and governments.

The new economic institutions of capitalism

Blockchains can be used by firms, but they can also replace firms. A ledger of contracts and capital can now be decentralised and distributed in a way they could not before. Ledgers of identity, permission, privilege and entitlement can be maintained and enforced without the need for government backing.

Institutional cryptoeconomics

This is what institutional cryptoeconomics studies: the institutional consequences of cryptographically secure and trustless ledgers.

Classical and neoclassical economists understand the purpose of economics as studying the production and distribution of scarce resources, and the factors which underpinned that production and distribution.

Institutional economics understands the economy as made of rules. Rules (like laws, languages, property rights, regulations, social norms, and ideologies) allow dispersed and opportunistic people to coordinate their activity together. Rules facilitate exchange — economic exchange but also social and political exchange as well.

What has come to be called cryptoeconomics focuses on the economic principles and theory underpinning the blockchain and alternative blockchain implementations. It looks at game theory and incentive design as they relate to blockchain mechanism design.

By contrast, institutional cryptoeconomics looks at the institutional economics of the blockchain and cryptoeconomy. Like its close cousin institutional economics, the economy is a system to coordinate exchange. But rather than looking at rules, institutional cryptoeconomics focuses on ledgers: data structured by rules.

Institutional cryptoeconomics is interested in the rules that govern ledgers, the social, political, and economic institutions that have developed to service those ledgers, and how the invention of the blockchain changes the patterns of ledgers throughout society.

The economic consequences of the blockchain

Institutional cryptoeconomics gives us the tools to understand what is happening in the blockchain revolution — and what we can't predict.

Blockchains are an experimental technology. Where the blockchain can be used is an entrepreneurial question. Some ledgers will move onto the blockchain. Some entrepreneurs will try to move ledgers onto the blockchain and fail. Not everything is a blockchain use case. We probably haven't yet seen the blockchain killer app. Nor can we predict what the combination of ledgers, cryptography, peer to peer networking will throw up in the future.

This process is going to be extremely disruptive. The global economy faces (what we expect will be) a lengthy period of uncertainty about how the facts that underpin it will be restructured, dismantled, and reorganised.

The best uses of the blockchain have to be 'discovered'. Then they have to be implemented in a real world political and economic system that has deep, established institutions that already service ledgers. That second part will not be cost free.

Ledgers are so pervasive — and the possible applications of the blockchain so all-encompassing — that some of the most fundamental principles governing our society are up for grabs.

Institutional creative destruction

We've been through revolutions like this before.

It is common to compare the invention of Bitcoin and the blockchain with the internet. The blockchain is Internet 2.0 — or Internet 4.0. The internet is a powerful tool that has revolutionised the way we interact and do business. But if anything the comparison undersells the blockchain. The internet has allowed us to communicate and exchange better — more quickly, more efficiently.

But the blockchain allows us to exchange differently. A better metaphor for the blockchain is the invention of mechanical time.

Before mechanical time, human activity was temporally regulated by nature: the crow of the rooster in the morning, the slow descent into darkness at night. As the economic historian Douglas W. Allen argues, the problem was variability: "there was simply too much variance in the measurement of time ... to have a useful meaning in many daily activities".

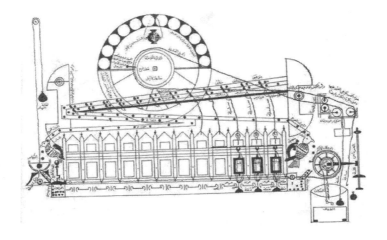

The 12th century Jayrun Water Clock

"The effect of the reduction in the variance of time measurement was felt everywhere", Allen writes. Mechanical time opened up entirely new categories of economic organisation that had until then been not just impossible, but unimaginable. Mechanical time allowed trade and exchange to be synchronised across great distances. It allowed for production and transport to be coordinated. It allowed for the day to be structured, for work to be compensated according to the amount of time worked — and for workers to know that they were being compensated fairly. Both employers and employees could look at a standard, independent instrument to verify that a contract had been performed. To understand this, just look at the first train that ran from London to Birmingham. It left at 9am and got there at 12:09pm. Except that the journey time was actually only 3 hours.

The extra 9 minutes was the difference between London time and Birmingham time. As a result, the railways made countries all operate on the same time – a huge leap forward.

Complete and incomplete smart contracts

Oliver Williamson and Ronald Coase (who was also an economics Nobel prize winner, in 1991) put contracts at the heart of economic and business organisation. Contracts are at the centre of institutional cryptoeconomics. It is here that blockchains have the most revolutionary implications.

Smart contracts on the blockchain allow for contractual agreements to be automatically, autonomously, and securely executed. Smart contracts can eliminate an entire class of work that currently maintains, enforces and confirms that contracts are executed — accountants, auditors, lawyers, and indeed much of the legal system.

But the smart contracts are limited by what can be specified in the algorithm. Economists have focused on the distinction between complete and incomplete contracts.

A complete contract specifies what is to occur under every possible contingency. An incomplete contract allows the terms of the contract to be renegotiated in the case of unexpected events. Incomplete contracts provide one explanation for why some exchanges take place in firms, and why others take place in markets, and provide a further guide to questions surrounding vertical integration and the size of the firm.

Complete contracts are impossible to execute, while incomplete contracts are expensive. The blockchain, through smart contracts, lowers the information costs and transactions costs associated with many incomplete contracts and so expands the scale and scope of economic activity that can be undertaken. It allows markets to operate where before only large firms could operate, and it allows businesses and markets to operate where before only government could operate.

The precise details of how and when this will occur is a challenge and a problem for entrepreneurs to resolve. Currently, oracles provide a link between the algorithmic world of the blockchain and the real world, trusted entities that convert information into data that can be processed by a smart contract.

The real gains to be made in the blockchain revolution, we suggest, are in developing better and more powerful oracles — converting incomplete contracts to contracts that are sufficiently complete to be written algorithmically and executed on the blockchain.

The merchant revolution of the middle ages was made possible by the development of merchant courts — effectively trusted oracles — that allowed traders to enforce agreements privately. For blockchain, that revolution seems yet to come.

Whither government?

The blockchain economy puts pressure on government processes in a whole host of ways, from taxation, to regulation, to service delivery.

Investigating these changes is an ongoing project of ours. But consider, for instance, how we regulate banks.

Prudential controls have evolved to ensure the safety and soundness of financial institutions that interact with the public. Typically these controls (for example, liquidity and capital requirements) have been justified by the fact that depositors and shareholders are unable to observe the bank's ledger. The depositors and shareholders are unable to discipline the firm and its management.

Bank runs occur when depositors discover (or simply imagine) that their bank might not be able to cover their deposits, and they rush to withdraw their money.

One possible application of the blockchain would allow depositors and shareholders to continuously monitor the bank's reserves and lendings, substantially eliminating the information asymmetries between them and the bank management.

In this world, market discipline would be possible. Public trust in the immutability of the blockchain would ensure no false bank runs occurred. The role of the regulator might be limited to certifying the blockchain was correctly and securely structured.

A more far reaching application would be a cryptobank — an autonomous blockchain application that borrows short and lends long, perhaps matching borrowers with lenders directly. A cryptobank structured algorithmically by smart contracts would have the same transparency properties as the bank with a public blockchain ledger but with other features that might completely neglect the need for regulators. For example, a cryptobank could be self-liquidating. At the moment the cryptobank began trading while insolvent, the underlying assets would be automatically disbursed to shareholders and depositors.

It is unclear what regulatory role government should have in this world.

Tyler Cowen and Alex Tabarrok have argued that much government regulation appears to be designed to resolve asymmetric information problems — problems that, in a world of information ubiquity, often do not exist any more. Blockchain applications significantly increase this information ubiquity, and make that information more transparent, permanent, and accessible.

Blockchains have their uses in what is being called 'regtech' — the application of technology to the traditional regulatory functions of auditing, compliance, and market surveillance. And we ought not to dismiss the possibility that there will be new economic problems that demand new consumer protections or market controls in the blockchain world.

Nevertheless, the restructuring and recreation of basic economic forms like banks will put pressure not just on how regulation is enforced, but what the regulation should do.

Whither Big Business?

The implications for big business are likely to be just as profound. Business size is often driven by the need to cover the costs of business hierarchy — in turn due to incomplete contracts and technological necessity of large scale financial investment. That business model has meant that shareholder capitalism is the dominant form of business organisation. The ability to write more complete contracts on the blockchain means that entrepreneurs and innovators will be able to maintain ownership and control of their human capital and profit at the same time. The nexus between operating a successful business and access to financial capital has been weakening over time, but now might even be broken. The age of human capitalism is dawning.

Entrepreneurs will be able to write a valuable app and release it into the "wild" ready to be employed by anyone and everyone who needs that functionality. The entrepreneur in turn simply observes micro-payments accumulating in their wallet. A designer could release their design into the "wild" and final consumers could download that design to their 3D printer and have the product almost immediately. This business model could see more (localised) manufacturing occur.

The ability of consumers to interact directly with producers or designers will limit the role that middlemen play in the economy. Logistics firms, however, will continue to prosper, but the advent of driverless transportation will see disruption to industry too.

Bear in mind, any disruption of business will also disrupt the company tax base. It may become difficult for government to tax business at all — so we might see greater pressure on sales (consumption) taxes and even poll taxes.

Conclusion

The blockchain and associated technological changes will massively disrupt current economic conditions. The industrial revolution ushered in a world where business models were predicated on hierarchy and financial capitalism. The blockchain revolution will see an economy dominated by human capitalism and greater individual autonomy.

How that unfolds is unclear at present. Entrepreneurs and innovators will resolve uncertainty, as always, through a process of trial and error. No doubt great fortunes will be made and lost before we know exactly how this disruption will unfold.

APPENDIX 14

Philosophical Teachings of Bitcoin

Here we split Bitcoin by topics, to result in three parts:

- I: Philosophical Teachings of Bitcoin
- II: Economic Teachings of Bitcoin
- III: Technological Teachings of Bitcoin

Lesson 1: Immutability and change

Bitcoin is inherently hard to describe. It is a new thing, and any attempt to draw a comparison to previous concepts — be it by calling it digital gold or the internet of money — is bound to fall short of the whole. Whatever your favourite analogy might be, two aspects of Bitcoin are absolutely essential: decentralization and immutability.

One way to think about Bitcoin is as an automated social contract. The software is just one piece of the puzzle, and hoping to change Bitcoin by changing the software is an exercise in futility. One would have to convince the rest of the network to adopt the changes, which is more a psychological effort than a software engineering one.

The following might sound absurd at first, like so many other things in this space, but I believe that it is profoundly true nonetheless: You won't change Bitcoin, but Bitcoin will change you.

"Bitcoin will change us more than we will change it." — Marty Bent

It took me a long time to realize the profundity of this. Since Bitcoin is just software and all of it is open-source, you can simply change things at will, right? Wrong. Very wrong. Unsurprisingly, Bitcoin's creator knew this all too well.

"The nature of Bitcoin is such that once version 0.1 was released, the core design was set in stone for the rest of its lifetime." — Satoshi Nakamoto

Many people have attempted to change Bitcoin's nature. So far all of them have failed. While there is an endless sea of forks and altcoins, the Bitcoin network still does its thing, just as it did when the first node went online. The altcoins won't matter in the long run. The forks will eventually starve to death. Bitcoin is what matters. As long as our fundamental understanding of mathematics and/or physics doesn't change, the Bitcoin honeybadger will continue to not care.

"Bitcoin is the first example of a new form of life. It lives and breathes on the internet. It lives because it can pay people to keep it alive. [...] It can't be changed. It can't be argued with. It can't be tampered with. It can't be corrupted. It can't be stopped. [...] If nuclear war destroyed half of our planet, it would continue to live, uncorrupted. " — Ralph Merkle

The heartbeat of the Bitcoin network will outlast all of ours.

Realising the above changed me way more than the past blocks of the Bitcoin blockchain ever will. It changed my time preference, my understanding of economics, my political views, and so much more. Hell, it is even changing people's diets. If all of this sounds crazy to you, you're in good company. All of this is crazy, and yet it is happening. Bitcoin taught me that it won't change. I will.

Lesson 2: The scarcity of scarcity

In general, the advance of technology seems to make things more abundant. More and more people are able to enjoy what previously have been luxurious goods. Soon, we will all live like kings. Most of us already do. As Peter Diamandis wrote in Abundance: "Technology is a resource-liberating mechanism. It can make the once scarce the now abundant."

Bitcoin, an advanced technology in itself, breaks this trend and creates a new commodity which is truly scarce. Some even argue that it is one of the scarcest things in the universe. The supply can't be inflated, no matter how much effort one chooses to expend towards creating more.

"Only two things are genuinely scarce: time and bitcoin." — Saifedean Ammous

Paradoxically, it does so by a mechanism of copying. Transactions are broadcast, blocks are propagated, the distributed ledger is — well, you guessed it — distributed. All of these are just fancy words for copying. Heck, Bitcoin even copies itself onto as many computers as it can, by incentivizing individual people to run full nodes and mine new blocks.

All of this duplication wonderfully works together in a concerted effort to produce scarcity.

In a time of abundance, Bitcoin taught me what real scarcity is.

Lesson 3: An immaculate conception

Everyone loves a good origin story. The origin story of Bitcoin is a fascinating one, and the details of it are more important than one might think at first. Who is Satoshi Nakamoto? Was he one person or a group of people? Was he a she? Time-traveling alien, or advanced AI? Outlandish theories aside, we will probably never know. And this is important.

atoshi chose to be anonymous. He planted the seed of Bitcoin. He stuck around for long enough to make sure the network won't die in its infancy. And then he vanished.

What might look like a weird anonymity stunt is actually crucial for a truly decentralized system. No centralized control. No centralized authority. No inventor. No-one to prosecute, torture, blackmail, or extort. An immaculate conception of technology.

"One of the greatest things that Satoshi did was disappear." — Jimmy Song

Since the birth of Bitcoin, thousands of other cryptocurrencies were created. None of these clones share its origin story. If you want to supersede Bitcoin, you will have to transcend its origin story. In a war of ideas, narratives dictate survival.

> "Gold was first fashioned into jewelry and used for barter over 7,000 years ago. Gold's captivating gleam led to it being considered a gift from the gods." — Gold: The Extraordinary Metal

Like gold in ancient times, Bitcoin might be considered a gift from the gods. Unlike gold, Bitcoins origins are all too human. And this time, we know who the gods of development and maintenance are: people all over the world, anonymous or not.

Bitcoin taught me that narratives are important.

Lesson 4: The problem of identity

Nic Carter, in an homage to Thomas Nagel's treatment of the same question in regards to a bat, wrote an excellent piece which discusses the following question: What is it like to be a bitcoin? He brilliantly shows that open, public blockchains in general, and Bitcoin in particular, suffer from the same conundrum as the Ship of Theseus: which Bitcoin is the real Bitcoin?

> "Consider just how little persistence Bitcoin's components have. The entire codebase has been reworked, altered, and expanded such that it

161

barely resembles its original version. [...] The registry of who owns what, the ledger itself, is virtually the only persistent trait of the network [...]

To be considered truly leaderless, you must surrender the easy solution of having an entity that can designate one chain as the legitimate one." — Nic Carter

It seems like the advancement of technology keeps forcing us to take these philosophical questions seriously. Sooner or later, self-driving cars will be faced with real-world versions of the trolley problem, forcing them to make ethical decisions about whose lives do matter and whose do not.

Cryptocurrencies, especially since the first contentious hard-fork, force us to think about and agree upon the metaphysics of identity. Interestingly, the two biggest examples we have so far have lead to two different answers. On August 1, 2017, Bitcoin split into two camps. The market decided that the unaltered chain is the original Bitcoin. One year earlier, on October 25, 2016, Ethereum split into two camps. The market decided that the alteredchain is the original Ethereum.

If properly decentralized, the questions posed by the Ship of Theseus will have to be answered in perpetuity for as long as these networks of value-transfer exist.

Bitcoin taught me that decentralization contradicts identity.

Lesson 5: Replication and locality

Quantum mechanics aside, locality is a non-issue in the physical world. The question "Where is X?" can be answered in a meaningful way, no matter if X is a person or an object. In the digital world, the question of where is already a tricky one, but not impossible to answer. Where are your emails, really? A bad answer would be "the cloud", which is just someone else's computer. Still, if you wanted to track down every storage device which has your emails on it you could, in theory, locate them.

With bitcoin, the question of "where" is really tricky. Where, exactly, are your bitcoins?

> "I opened my eyes, looked around, and asked the inevitable, the traditional, the lamentably hackneyed postoperative question: 'Where am I?'"
> — Daniel Dennett

The problem is twofold: First, the distributed ledger is distributed by full replication, meaning the ledger is everywhere. Second, there are no bitcoins. Not only physically, but technically.

Bitcoin keeps track of a set of unspent transaction outputs, without ever having to refer to an entity which represents a bitcoin. The existence of a bitcoin is inferred by looking at the set of unspent transaction outputs and calling every entry with a 100 million base units a bitcoin.

> "Where is it, at this moment, in transit? [...] First, there are no bitcoins. There just aren't. They don't

exist. There are ledger entries in a ledger that's shared [...] They don't exist in any physical location. The ledger exists in every physical location, essentially. Geography doesn't make sense here — it is not going to help you figuring out your policy here."
— Peter Van Valkenburgh

So, what do you actually own when you say "I have a bitcoin" if there are no bitcoins? Well, remember all these strange words which you were forced to write down by the wallet you used? Turns out these magic words are what you own: a magic spell which can be used to add some entries to the public ledger — the keys to "move" some bitcoins. This is why, for all intents and purposes, your private keys are your bitcoins. If you think I'm making all of this up feel free to send me your private keys.

Bitcoin taught me that locality is a tricky business.

Lesson 6: The power of free speech

Bitcoin is an idea. An idea which, in its current form, is the manifestation of a machinery purely powered by text. Every aspect of Bitcoin is text: The whitepaper is text. The software which is run by its nodes is text. The ledger is text. Transactions are text. Public and private keys are text. Every aspect of Bitcoin is text, and thus equivalent to speech.

"Congress shall make no law respecting an

establishment of religion, or prohibiting the free exercise thereof; or abridging the freedom of speech, or of the press; or the right of the people peaceably to assemble, and to petition the Government for a redress of grievances."
— First Amendment to the United States Constitution

Although the final battle of the Crypto Wars has not been fought yet, it will be very difficult to criminalize an idea, let alone an idea which is based on the exchange of text messages. Every time a government tries to outlaw text or speech, we slip down a path of absurdity which inevitably leads to abominations like illegal numbers and illegal primes.

As long as there is a part of the world where speech is free as in freedom, Bitcoin is unstoppable.

"There is no point in any Bitcoin transaction that Bitcoin ceases to be text. It is all text, all the time. [...]

Bitcoin is text. Bitcoin is speech. It cannot be regulated in a free country like the USA with guaranteed inalienable rights and a First Amendment that explicitly excludes the act of publishing from government oversight." — Beautyon

Bitcoin taught me that in a free society, free speech and free software are unstoppable.

Lesson 7: The limits of knowledge

Getting into Bitcoin is a humbling experience. I thought that I knew things. I thought that I was educated. I thought that I knew my computer science, at the very least. I studied it for years, so I have to know everything about digital signatures, hashes, encryption, operational security, and networks, right?

Wrong.

Learning all the fundamentals which make Bitcoin work is hard. Understanding all of them deeply is borderline impossible.

> "No one has found the bottom of the Bitcoin rabbit hole." — Jameson Lopp

My list of books to read keeps expanding way quicker than I could possibly read them. The list of papers and articles to read is virtually endless. There are more podcasts on all of these topics than I could ever listen to. It truly is humbling. Further, Bitcoin is evolving and it's almost impossible to stay up-to-date with the accelerating rate of innovation. The dust of the first layer hasn't even settled yet, and people have already built the second layer and are working on the third.

Bitcoin taught me that I know very little about almost anything. It taught me that this rabbit hole is bottomless.

Conclusion

Bitcoin is a child of the internet. Even though it requires computers to function efficiently, computer science is not sufficient to understand it. The implications of this new technology are far-reaching. Bitcoin is not only borderless but also boundaryless in respect to academic disciplines.

In this first part of the Teachings of Bitcoin I tried to outline some of the philosophical implications of this fascinating machinery. In part two I will try to discuss what Bitcoin taught me about economics. Part three will conclude this series to show what I, a technologist, have learned from the tech perspective by stumbling into Bitcoin.

As mentioned above, I think that any answer to the question "What have you learned from Bitcoin?" will always be incomplete. The systems are too dynamic, the space moving too fast, and the topics too numerous. Politics, game theory, monetary history, network theory, finance, cryptography, information theory, censorship, law and regulation, human organization, psychology — all these and more are areas of expertise which might help to grasp what Bitcoin is.

What have you learned from Bitcoin?

APPENDIX 16

NFTs

NFTs —what are they and how do they work, who uses them, where can you get them? How to start trading in them.

What are NFTs?

NFT's also known as Non-Fungible Tokens, are digital assets that represents real-world objects like art, music, games, videos, and other collectables. These digital assets are bought and sold online, with the increased popularity of cryptocurrencies. They generally use the same technology as cryptocurrencies such as Ethereum and many of the NFT platforms are Ethereum platform based with the vast majority built using one of two Ethereum token standards (ERC-721 and ERC-1155).

Using blockchain technology allows a buyer to prove ownership of the piece of digital art as it is cryptographically signed, and this proves that the item purchased is genuine and the owner is verified. NFTs have been around since 2014 and are gaining popularity now because they are becoming an increasingly fashionable way to buy and sell digital artwork. The total value of NFT sales in 2020 was in the region of $250 million, although the total value of NFT sales in the first quarter of 2021 alone, was arounf $2 billion (Source: cloudwards.net)

How Do they Work?

The actual content of most NFTs are not located on the blockchain as this would take up too much space. Instead, there is a link to where the NFT is located. This link will take the owner to the actual NFT purchased such as a piece of music, a song or an item of digital art and it means this cryptographic link to the blockchain acts a bit like a certificate of authenticity keeping track of who is the original owner. This cannot be faked as it has a signature that proves that the digital asset is 100% genuine.

Who uses NFTs?

NFTs are considered beneficial in a wide variety of use cases. The most popular use cases are digital art, fashion, licenses and certifications, collectibles, itemiused sports game tickets, name services and domains, the monetisation of virtual land in virtual worlds, and other game services and components, and in gaming, elements and items can be tokenised and exchanged. Four of the main use cases are described here.

Art: a digital artist, Beeple, recently sold an NFT of his artwork for a massive $69 million at Christie's auction house, which created waves throughout the blockchain space. This eye opening NFT sale came after a series of increasingly valuable auctions. The artist Beeple sold his first series of NFT's in October 2020, with two pieces priced at $66,666.66 each. He then sold a group of his works for around $3.5 million. Christie's auction house presents a legitimate value for Beeple's art as well as NFT as a technology.

Fashion: Blockchain technology has been able to blend seamlessly in the fashion world. Buyers can easily verify the ownership of their purchased items and accessories digitally, therefore reducing the risk of counterfeit goods being received for large sums. Consumers can simply scan a simple QR code on the price tag or ownership documentation, which will verify with the digital cryptographic signature stored on the blockchain.

Licenses and Certifications: NFT use cases can also provide astute benefits for verifying licensing and certifications. A good example is course completion certificates, such as a Batchelors or Master's degree certificate or license, are generally presented to successful candidates in paper or more recently digital form.

Universities, colleges, and employers ask for replicas of the course completion document as proof before they offer a position to someone in a company or an institute. These certifications or licenses are therefore digitally signed and linked back to the blockchain where a unique signature is generated and stored, providing verification of that document.

Collectibles: collectibles are one of the profound entries among use cases of an NFT. These online collectibles such as Cryptokitties were one of the original ways in which people found out about the use of NFTs. The popularity of Cryptokitties gained prominence in 2017 as they congested the Ethereum network.

Where can you get them?

Here are five websites who let you buy digital assets using NFT technology:

rarible.com is a community owned NFT website which showcases 20,000 collectors and creators, which has its own management token called RARI, which it distributes to its Rarible community members.

niftygateway.com is an ultra-exclusive platform where Nifties are the first to know about exclusive drops from artists, athletes, brands, and creators. Drops are sold directly by creators such as T.J. Miller and Steve Aoki, with the possibility to be re-sold on Nifty Gateway's own secondary market. In contrast to other NFT marketplaces, Nifty Gateway allows bids to be made in USD from your credit card.

opensea.io is the largest NFT marketplace for digital goods. It specializes in 200 categories of digital assets that include gaming items, domain names, collectibles, and art. The primary form of payment is Ethereum, however, Open Sea accepts payment in a number of other cryptocurrencies as well.

foundation.app is a provider that made its mark when a fierce bidding war fetched $580,000 for Nyan Cat. Having prominence of "The New

Creative Economy," Foundation aims to bring together digital creators, cryptocurrency enthusiasts, and collectors where its users can browse digital artwork and featured creators allowing bids, which are made in Ethereum which is held in MetaMask (the cryptocurrency wallet Foundation recommends).

makersplace.com is a rare digital art platform, collating original digital creations from the world's most creative individuals. It helps digital creators protect and sell limited edition digital works to fans and collectors. It is easily accessible to anyone who does not have any cryptocurrency assets and has partnered with Stripe to provide secure credit card payments around the world.

How to Start Trading in NFTs

NFT marketplaces are just some of Ethereum's dApps. They allow you to create, sell, and buy NFTs.

The first thing you do is get an Ethereum wallet and some Ethereum which most Scotcoin users will have. If not then go to **metamask.io** and either install the web browser plug-in (which supports all major browsers such as Google Chrome, Brave and Mozilla Firefox) or download the Metamask app on your smartphone; then you create a new wallet and carefully write down your 12 or 24 word passphrase or login using your existing 12 or 24 word passphrase.

Secondly, buy some Ethereum. You may already have

some, if not then you can buy Ethereum inside your Metamask wallet by simply clicking on the "buy" button and buy using the Transak service using bank transfer or a debit card or use an exchange of your choice such as Coinbase or Bittrex.

Once you have your Ethereum wallet, preferably via metamask.io and some Ethereum in the wallet you are ready to start selling and buying NFTs.

There are several marketplaces and some are described in the previous section. For this example, we will use opensea.io and the first thing you do is sign up for new user's account or sign in if you are an existing user, and connect your Metamask wallet using the connect wallet button. To start creating a collection it asks you to click on "sign" to sign a digital signature and create a secure entry on the Ethereum Mainnet blockchain and then create a collection and add images to the collection, then finally the step which again connects to your Metamask wallet, takes an amount of Ethereum to pay for the opensea.io service.

Further reading:

NFTS Explained: What Are Non-Fungible Tokens and How Do They Work? https://beincrypto.com/learn/nfts-explainer/

What is an NFT? Non-fungible tokens explained, and why you shouldn't dismiss this fad https://www.techradar.com/news/what-is-an-nft-non-fungible-tokens-explained-and-why-you-shouldnt-dismiss-this-fad

NFTs And Their Use Cases: A Complete Guide
https://101blockchains.com/nft-use-cases/

Article by Brian Mackay – Cybersecurity consultant and technical support for The Scotcoin Project CIC. Twitter: @BrianMackaythurso

APPENDIX 17

Decentralised Finance

Decentralised finance (known as DeFi) is a blockchain-based form of finance that doesn't rely on central financial intermediaries such as exchanges, or banks to offer traditional financial instruments, and instead uses smart contracts on blockchains to ensure transactions are safe.

DeFi platforms allow people to lend or borrow funds from others, speculate on price movements on a range of assets using derivatives, trade cryptocurrencies, insure against risks, and earn interest in savings-like accounts. DeFi uses a layered architecture and highly composable building blocks.

The current financial system is what we would call 'centralised' — it is not only potentially outdated and highly manipulated, but it creates costly fees, is inefficient, and open to, deception, fraud and corruption by those who have access to that central control.

Blockchain technologies have led to a new decentralised financial system, which is working towards a low-cost, fast, efficient, trustworthy, completely transparent global financial system, without a central authority that is accessible to everyone around the world

DeFi's foundation is the blockchain tech — but how can this new system achieve what the old one couldn't?

Before the Blockchain, the financial system was run by people, whereas now the entire system can be based on mathematics and computer science. Blockchain Technology is the cornerstone of DeFi, and is what makes the decentralised part of it possible

The best way to understand what is meant by the term blockchain is to split up the word. Block and Chain. A block is a list of transactions, and a block is complete when all the useable space in the list is used up. Then the Blocks of data are linked to a previous block of transaction data. So a Blockchain is a series of blocks of transaction data linked together.

There are three pillars of blockchain technology that make it unique:

Decentralisation — The Data is stored in multiple locations, on multiple computers around the world. No one person, corporation, government, authority or entity can control any aspect of the data recording or storage process. Any changes to the open source software and the blockchain protocol has to go through a consensus process, which no one person, company or government has control over — and so this ensures its integrity.

Transparency — All transaction data is recorded on a public ledger that is available for everyone to see, so there is no way to fabricate transaction data or conceal any transactions. If the government were to use DeFi then every one of its citizens could see exactly where each penny of their taxes is going.

Immutability — The data on the blockchain cannot be changed, forged or altered. This is because once data is verified it is unmodifiable, because it is distributed across a network of computers across the world, making it hard to destroy or edit. In fact, no one entity controls the data or the network, thus making the whole process transparent.

DeFi's Ecosystem — Ethereum

Bitcoin and Etherium have different uses. Bitcoin is a currency that can be used to buy things, transfer or store value, while Etherium is a programmable blockchain that people can build software on to create valuable products and services.

Due to the decentralised properties of blockchain technology the software that people can build on Ethereum are called Decentralised Applications (DAPPS)

The DeFi system wants to turn the global financial system into a more transparent and trustworthy one.

But how can it work without a centralised authority?

Ether was created as a form of payment which essentially exists to incentivise people to run the Etherium network. Each participating person around the world, and their computer, is a node on the network, and each time they process and publish transaction data on the Ethereum blockchain they are rewarded with Ether. Ether is a lot like Bitcoin, as it is a currency that can be used to buy things, trade or store value.

Everyone who wants to start a DAPP on the Ethereum Network has to pay for the computing power and the space required using Ether.

The cost of which is determined by a built-in pricing system known as Gas.

Transaction data can contain value in the form of Ether and information in the form of code.

The layer on top of the base hardware layer, previously spoken about, is the software layer.

This software layer supports a programming language library that consists of language such as Solidity, Vyper and more. Using these languages developers can write what are called Smart Contracts — lines of code that dictate the terms of a contract and control the execution of the contract.

Both the Hardware and Software Layer creates the perfect trustworthy digital environment for making and executing smart contracts.

Smart contracts have the unique ability to authorise transactions and carry out terms of contracts within a trusted environment, which eliminates the need for a central authority.

Indeed, smart contracts make transactions trackable, transparent and permanent.

Both the Software and Hardware layers when combined essentially make a global decentralised super computer, known as the Ethereum Virtual Machine (EVM).

The final layer of Ethereum is the Application Layer which is where people can build and launch third party decentralised applications (DAPPS). These are decentralised because they operate on Ethereum's decentralised blockchain platform. A good example of a DAPP is CryptoKitties.

DeFi's Financial Stack

There are five main components:

Stablecoins: Each cryptocurrency has a different function or utility, ones that fix their price to something like the Dollar, are known as Stable Coins. They were designed to bridge the gap between Fiat currencies and crypto currencies, and reducing the volatility associated with crypto.

Exchanges: Commonly referred to as DEXs (Decentralised Exchanges), they allow users to swap cryptocurrencies for other cryptocurrencies, on a peer-to-peer basis without a centralised authority. These offer low fees, security, over-collateralisation and control to its users.

Money Markets: These markets are able to facilitate both lending ands borrowing, and they provide liquidity which is essential to any financial market. Lending your crypto for interest is a great way to earn passive income on idle assets. DeFi money markets like Compound use a Liquidity Pool Model — instead of lending your cryptocurrency to someone directly it is put in a pool with other users' funds, and those who want a loan will get an interest rate that is based on supply and demand. DeFi Money markets are completely transparent. There are no credit scores or credit histories associated with its users which ensures privacy for its users; instead in order to secure a loan borrowers use Collateralised Debt Positions (CDP) which is similar to how you are able to lean against your house or take out a loan secured by an asset as collateral.

Synthetics: This is a term used in finance to describe an asset that is designed to behave like another asset, except with some specific changes to the assets behaviour. In finance, synthetic products are derivatives, which are assets whose value is derived from and dependent on the value of another asset. These include options, swaps and futures contracts. They exist because they offer investors highly customisable options that provide certain risk exposure and cash-flow patterns. The current centralised synthetic asset market value is around $1,200,000,000,000,000. In DeFi, synthetics are tokens that follow the price of another token, and are used to facilitate funding, liquidity creation and market access while offering complete transparency and superior security. This part of DeFi's financial stack is extremely complex and can expose users to high levels of risk.

Insurance: Insurance is used to mitigate risk and

protect people from certain types of losses. Using Decentralised Insurance, i.e. without insurance companies, crypto holders can provide insurance in exchange for interest, or they can buy insurance. DeFi projects that currently offer insurance include Nexus Mutual and Opyn. Essentially decentralised insurance acts as a safeguard against hacks, glitches and bugs, ensuring the crypto holders feel secure operating in this new financial ecosystem.

Visit Scotcoin:

SCOTCOINPROJECT.COM

In 2021, readers of Temple Melville's BLOCKCHAIN, BITCOIN AND YOU may still be able to claim 1,000 FREE Scotcoin as a part of their purchase of this book, either in paperback or electronic form. To find out if you can claim 1,000 free Scotcoin, sent to your nominated cryptocurrency wallet, write to:

peter@leamingtonbooks.com

quoting SCOT2021 and where you bought the book from (eg Amazon), and you will hear back from The Scotcoin Project CIC by email.